The
Great Intimidators

Also by Gerald Sparrow

Autobiography and Travel

LAND OF THE MOONFLOWER
OPIUM VENTURE
RETURN TICKET
THE STAR SAPPHIRES
LAWYER AT LARGE
NOT WISELY, BUT TOO WELL
NO OTHER ELEPHANT
THE GOLDEN ORCHID
CONFESSIONS OF AN ECCENTRIC

Biography

GORDON: MANDARIN AND PASHA
'R.A.B.': STUDY OF A STATESMAN
HUSSEIN OF JORDAN

Criminology

MURDER PARADE
THE GREAT SWINDLERS
THE GREAT IMPOSTORS
THE GREAT FORGERS
THE GREAT ABDUCTORS
THE GREAT TRAITORS
THE GREAT DECEIVERS
THE GREAT ASSASSINS
THE GREAT DEFENDERS
THE GREAT SPIES
THE GREAT CONSPIRATORS
THE GREAT DEFAMERS
VINTAGE VICTORIAN MURDER
VINTAGE EDWARDIAN MURDER
SATAN'S CHILDREN

Tourism

VISITING EGYPT
VISITING LIBYA
VISITING GREECE

Modern Politics

THE SPHINX AWAKES
MODERN JORDAN

Satire

HOW TO BECOME AN M.P.
HOW TO BECOME A MILLIONAIRE

071. 75

The
Great Intimidators

JUDGE
GERALD SPARROW

JOHN LONG
London

JOHN LONG LIMITED
3 Fitzroy Square, London W1

AN IMPRINT OF THE HUTCHINSON GROUP

London Melbourne Sydney Auckland
Wellington Johannesburg Cape Town
and agencies throughout the world

First published 1972

BARNSLEY
PUBLIC LIBRARY
ACC. A84165
CLASS H364.1
CAT.
CHECK 13. MAR. 1972

© Gerald Sparrow 1972

*This book has been set in Times type, printed in Great Britain
on antique wove paper by Anchor Press, and
bound by Wm. Brendon, both of Tiptree, Essex*

ISBN 0 09 109500 X

Contents

TO
Chaluey

Author to Reader

'Very softly down a glade runs a waiting, watching shade,
And the whisper spreads and widens far and near.
And the sweat is on thy brow, for he passes even now—
He is Fear, oh little hunter, he is Fear.'

WE have called this book *The Great Intimidators*. That was a title suggested by my publishers and immediately agreed to by me because we thought that it was exactly right. Without any unnecessary cleverness it tells the whole story of this book. The theme is to show the intimidation that exists in the world today with some examples from the past.

We are concerned with dramatic personal intimidation of one man by another, as in the case of Prince Hari Singh, we are concerned with the intimidation of minorities by majorities, and, the most recent manifestation, the attempted intimidation of majorities by well-organised and vociferous minorities. We think that the growth of intimidation strikes at the very roots of democratic government, with its rights of free worship, free speech, a free press, and freedom from arrest where no crime has been committed.

We think it strange and sinister that in the 1970s intimidation—the attempt to cow people, to make them timid or afraid so that they will do what you want them to do—appears actually to be a waxing and not a waning force. It is clear that the fascist–communist states accept intimidation as a political weapon. If you are a writer in the Soviet Union, and are critical of the rich, privileged bureaucracy of the communist hierarchy, you go to a slave-labour camp, or are declared insane in a mockery of a medical investigation that chills the spectators with its ingenious horror.

If you are a Chinese and think that the little red book of the poor old current Emperor of China is a load of codswallop, and say so, you will be 'reformed' in prison for years, without a trial, and with no certain date of release. These were in effect the methods employed by Hitler. Although economically communism and fascism have a different approach, in the way they exercise power through fear they are exactly similar.

So we depict in this book not only the private intimidators but the public intimidators as well. Fear and the manipulation of fear—which is intimidation—has become not only a political weapon increasingly used. It has also become big business. The girl who smells until she realises that *Whiffo* will cure that little disability, so that she becomes radiant and confident like Sybil the *femme fatale*, is putting fear into advertising terms. The message is: 'You may smell. This should scare the panties off you, for it is fatal to catching a lover or securing a husband. So you really must buy *Whiffo*—now.'

Poor cold Harry wandering the icy streets is much to be despised. He may be saving on his fuel bill, but he is not a regular fellow. Why can't he buy one—or two—of our lovely economical units and bask in the winter warmth with his wife and kids like the other Joneses? And having done that, buy an additional hot-water heater and really be in the swim? The message is that poor cold Harry is a nitwit, that he does not know the ropes. Don't be like poor cold Harry.

And, finally, you ageing dodderer, you are losing your sexual powers. You say you don't mind? Don't be ridiculous. Of course you mind. *Viro* will put the juices back for you. Women will hanker after you again. Your hair will be more luxuriant, your steady sexual gaze will make female heads turn. Sex, sex, sex is the real reason for living. Join the crowd again. *Viro* will enable you to flex your sexual muscles again. The message is that you need despair no longer. You need not fear impotence. *Viro* will banish your growing sexual fear and frustration.

Happy Christmas, everybody! Post unnecessarily early for

the convenience of the Post Office. Otherwise your mail may arrive too late.

A little exaggerated? Yes. But containing many grains of truth that should make us think.

Let us look for a moment at crime. The old theory was that people stole and committed other crimes mainly because they were poor and hungry, often destitute. This theory is now reluctantly discarded because it has become obvious that the more money people have the more effectively they organise for crime. Bank hold-ups and the robbing of security vans have now in Britain—as in America—become big business. And the methods used for bringing off these dangerous coups are the intimidation of those in charge of the money by every device open to the criminal. A shot is fired over the bank counter. That shot means: 'Hand over the money or you've had it!' The acid sprayed into the eyes of security guards so that their flesh will burn or they will lose their sight or both—this is the direct command. Hand over or suffer burning and blindness.

Then, of course, we have political intimidation. Oddly enough in Britain there is virtually no intimidation of the new Left by the Right. That will come. At present communist headquarters in London are as unmolested as Church House. Communist meetings are ignored and undisturbed. It may perhaps irritate the brothers that the public do not regard them as a serious menace—and it may be a mistake. At present it is the little organised groups of hoodlums, often from the universities, who—adopting the techniques of the Hitler youth and perverting these techniques to the purpose of anarchy—are finding that intimidation in Britain pays off for the time being, until the backlash comes.

Perhaps I shall not bore you if I tell you of a personal experience of this a short time ago. We had a private political meeting on southern Africa in the Arlington Hotel, Brighton. Three speeches were made, all studiously moderate in tone. A crowd of organised louts surrounded the entrance to the hotel. They wanted to attend—and wreck—the meeting. Infuriated that they were unable to do so, they were determined to mob the speakers as they left and intimidate them with insults and a violent demonstration.

As we came out a howling mob, giving the Nazi salute and shouting 'Pigs' and 'Sharpville', tried to claw the speakers. Only the magnificently tolerant and effective police saved us. This was England 1970. Four of the culprits were arrested, complaining of course of 'police brutality'. The message here was clear. No one shall express a view on southern Africa in public that conflicts with the view of the New Left and the communists. They were saying: 'We spit on free speech, as we spit on you.' As this kind of behaviour becomes more and more common the political pattern behind it will emerge and we shall wake up one morning, as France did so recently, to discover that the rebels and the prophets of anarchy have taken over the streets. This, it seems, is the new age of intimidation.

Of course, intimidation these days is not universally confined to one side. There are military dictatorships where the police use torture to extract confessions and this is intimidation at its most horrific. But the alarming prospect is that intimidation is so far meeting with success—and nothing is so certain to be pursued as proven success in achieving objectives.

In the summer of 1970 an important cricket tour was cancelled because the 'radical' Left threatened 'trouble'. When Mr. Wilson wanted to declare wildcat strikes illegal the trade unions came out in open intimidation of the government. 'Do you want to split the Labour movement?' The act was abandoned and Mrs. Castle was left holding a banished baby.

Negotiation and compromise, in which the British used to excel and which they exported to the world as an invisible benefit, are very much out of favour. Negotiation without threats, we are told, never gets you anywhere. And there is some evidence to support this contention. Writers and authors in Britain have been pleading for years with the authorities for a small payment on the use of the books in public libraries, on the same lines that musical and dramatic works are protected. They have got nowhere at all. Ministers smile and shuffle and do nothing. The Society of Authors is a gentlemanly body, and gentlemen these days do not get what they want and deserve. It is the age of the well-organised bully-boy.

The growth of intimidation in so many fields is, I suggest, a much more immediate and sinister development than the growth of permissive behaviour. It may be a mistake to allow the sodomists to cavort around corrupting the youth of the country, and it may be unwise to give sexual instruction to the very young people who have perfectly normal and decent instincts until sex is put up graphically by a teacher on a blackboard. The current vogue for dirt and drugs may shock those who were brought up on whisky, beer and soap. But this permissiveness is a phase. It is a rebellion against the former hero, the English gentleman, with his ridiculous code of honour, ethics and well-cut suits. The new half-educated young feel inferior and this leads to aggressive behaviour to assert themselves as individuals. All this is not unnatural and not wholly bad. Long hair was the vogue in the eighteenth century, and dirt was regarded as a sign of holiness in the Middle Ages. So the modern adoption of these outward signs of a cult may be reactionary, but they are not in themselves new and certainly not dangerous.

Intimidation is a much more powerful and evil weapon. Psychologists rightly regard fear as the most common human failing. Fear resides in each of us, subdued but never absent. It has come down to us from our earliest times. Dogs eat with their tails down. Although no one has ever taken away their food, in their previous wild existence they had to guard their food with their lives. So it is with us. We are all born and for ever remain fearful creatures. Courage, the conqueror of fear, is a fairly rare commodity. That is why it is the king of the virtues.

Finally, hoping that after this short introduction you will come along with me and read the chapters of this book, each of which deals with an example or aspect of intimidation, I would like to mention one development that certainly exists in Britain and, I think, is very slowly becoming operative in America and more quickly in Europe.

I mean the constant repetition of a false position until 'everyone' believes it. This, of course, was another well-tried Hitler and Goebbels' technique. We say, again and again and again, that the establishment is rotten, that capitalism is the robbing of the poor by the rich, that sexual freedom is good in itself, that marriage is very old hat, that society as it is must be destroyed and replaced by anarchy in which people will live as they want, and slowly more and more people come to accept the lie. And this method can be endlessly applied. 'All white South Africans are monsters.' 'Chairman Mao is the prophet of the twentieth century.' 'The Soviet Union never threatens anyone, least of all Hungary or Czecho-slovakia.' Repeat it and repeat it, and persuade the people that these are the new views to guide and formulate our tomorrows.

Some of these cries have already been accepted. In the film *Oh What a Lovely War!* we are told by implication that a whole generation of young men in the first world war were conned into fighting by a cynical and corrupt establishment. They died so that freedom might live? Don't make me laugh.

So the aim of the new intimidation is to employ violence and ridicule to make alien ideas fashionable.

This great turbulence, this gigantic clash of ideologies and the whole approach to life and living seems to me to make this an exciting age to live in. I revel in it.

But I think that, if there is a Satan watching what is happening to such civilisation as we have achieved, he must be chuckling.

America, the Soviet Union and Britain fought two wars in defence of their countries. In the case of Britain and America the abolition of fear was a paramount and unwritten war aim. We lost, in all, over four million lives, to achieve this. And now twenty-five years later, fear is back again, permeating our lives. The big computerised father knows all about you. Do not offend him. Conform. Be fashionable. Buy, eat and believe the right things. Or suffer.

Whatever view you may take of current events, here is a theme that is of immense current interest. It will shape the world we live in during the 'seventies and the years that follow.

2

Intimidation by Torture

WE are apt to think of torture—the infliction of acute pain by various means in order to terrify, to extort, or to extract confessions—as being very un-English. This is a complete illusion. Torture up to the seventeenth century was part of the royal prerogative and, as such, was not subject to any of the rules, controls and modifications by which it was contained in European judicial systems where it was part of the law of the land and subject to strict legal provisions.

It came as a shock to humanity that during Hitler's regime the Nazis tortured the Jews and then murdered them *en masse,* but it was the Japanese who, in 1941, reintroduced torture as a method of government. The Japanese leaders suddenly found themselves in control of a vast empire, stretching from Manchuria almost to Australia, with nearly a thousand million subjects. They were fighting a war against American, British and Commonwealth forces and they were determined not to tolerate any trouble in the occupied territories. To ensure this, their first step on entering a new country was to set up torture chambers. For instance, in the city of Bangkok they created three such places, one at Sapatum police station, one at Sala Daeng House, and one at the former residence of the manager of the Hong Kong Bank. In these torture chambers political trouble-makers, anyone suspected of espionage or sabotage and all persons accused of stealing Japanese property were tortured. The methods used were varied, but the favourite ones were the extraction of finger-nails, the burning of the most sensitive parts of the body, electric shock, and the inflation of the stomach by forcing water down the victim's throat, after which the stomach was jumped upon by a man wearing boots. The agonised cries of those being subjected to this treatment could be heard by the public passing any of these torture centres. This also was deliberate policy, a hint to the public that if they got into trouble they would receive similar treatment.

All this occurred only thirty years ago, so that we would be over-optimistic if we thought that torture was dead in the modern world—and indeed the extraordinary case which is the subject of this chapter shows that intimidation by torture was carried on in London a very few years ago by a gang of extortionists who found it an extremely effective weapon in their armoury.

Before we examine this extraordinary case let me justify my remark that torture is in a special sense an indigenous English product as far as European countries are concerned. Possibly we never developed quite the gift for horror that came naturally to the Chinese, who would arrange for a man to be slowly eaten to death by gnawing rats, but all torture is abhorrent and English torture was as terrible as any, for it was carried out by a people who regarded themselves as civilised and who were certainly at the time religiouslyminded.

The Greeks used torture in ancient Athens, but only against slaves, who, of course, had no civil rights. This seems to indicate that they regarded torture as improper and degrading if applied to a citizen. Likewise Roman law allowed the torture of slaves, but again torture was not used against citizens of Rome. It was, however, used against captives and prisoners of the Roman conquest.

In most German cities judicial torture was unknown until the end of the fourteenth century. In the statutes of the Italian municipalities we read of lawful torture much earlier. Torture continued in most European countries until the middle of the eighteenth century. In France the *question preparatoire* was continued until 1780 and torture in the French empire was not abolished until 1789. In Russia the Empress Catherine recommended the abolition of torture in 1763, but its practice was so universal and so much approved by the Russian establishment that it was not abolished until early in the nineteenth century. Long after that serfs were horse-whipped or beaten if they were rude or troublesome. In Austria, Prussia and Saxony torture was 'suspended' in the middle of the eighteenth century rather in the same way that we have suspended capital punishment today, but in fact in Bavaria and Hanover, and in some of the smaller principalities, torture lingered on until the end of the eighteenth century. In Scotland it was not until the reign of Queen Anne that an act was passed which said that 'No person accused of any crime in Scotland shall be subject or liable to any torture.'

From the year 1468 until the Commonwealth the practice of torture was frequent in England and is recorded in council books, and many torture warrants still exist. It died out, however, in the middle of the seventeenth century, condemned by the judges and the lawyers but lingering on as part of the prerogative. Although torture was not allowed by the statute law or the common law after 1650, the King's Prerogative retained torture in the case of special crime affecting the security of the state, such as treason and sedition. These special tortures were carried out by the servants of the Crown outside the judicial system on direct instructions from the monarch or his competent minister.

This prerogative of torture for centuries had been regarded as being independent of and indeed paramount to the common law of the land. The rolls of Parliament of 1292 establish this view and for many centuries the application of torture in England, in such cases as we have referred to, was carried out on warrants issued immediately by the king or by the Privy Council. The consequence was that in no country was torture so dangerous an instrument of power as in England. In other countries, where it was part of the system of trial, it was subject to rules and restrictions, fixed and determined by the law; but in England there were no rules, no law beyond the will of the Crown.

Perhaps when we realise that this was the position in England it will help us to understand how it could be that torture was used for centuries as a religious instrument. Just as the secular power in England, exercising the prerogative, was saying in effect to the traitor: 'You have betrayed

B

your country,' so religious leaders who ordered the torture of 'heretics' were saying: 'You have betrayed your faith.' This does not, of course, excuse the horrible history of torture, but it may, perhaps, in part explain it.

Torture seems to be a virulent and indestructible part of the pattern of human behaviour. There was certainly much more torture in the world between 1935 and 1945 than there had been during the previous one hundred and fifty years. One is almost tempted to say that torture is endemic. Nevertheless, in normal times, the modern world regards torture with absolute horror and cannot believe that it is still deliberately practised anywhere, certainly not in the city of London.

It therefore came as an outrageous shock to the public when a gang of business men, headed by Charles William Richardson, who was thirty-three, were charged before Mr. Justice Lawton on June 8th, 1967, with a whole series of crimes which showed that they had deliberately adopted torture as an instrument of extortion and that not once, but many times, they had tortured victims who were reluctant to give them what they demanded.

The charges related to transactions large and small which the prosecution believed they could prove. For instance, Jack Duval had been beaten up and forced to surrender two hundred dollars, a watch and a ring; Bernard Wajcemberg had been threatened with torture unless he paid the gang five thousand pounds. Similar threats were made against James Taggart; while 'grievous bodily harm' was inflicted on a number of people, including Derek Harris, Bernard Bridges, Benjamin Coulston, as well as Taggart, Alfred Blore and again Jack Duval.

Counsel for the Crown opened the case for the prosecution with these words: 'This case involves acts of brutal violence systematically inflicted deliberately and cold-bloodedly with utter ruthlessness. The case for the Crown is that the men in the dock are members of a gang of thugs under the leadership of Charles Richardson, whose policy and practice over a number of years was to enforce his will by violence and intimidation. The principal object of the gang's policy was to secure for Charles Richardson the absolute domination of a somewhat disreputable business.'

Although the Crown referred to the business of the gang as being disreputable, it was by no means negligible. Richardson's firm was registered. It had directors and board meetings. It carried on a certain amount of legitimate business in Britain and abroad and it was, perhaps, the reluctance of the police to interfere with what appeared to be business activities and a respectable façade that delayed the prosecution of Richardson and his gangsters longer than was strictly necessary. For instance, Richardson's firm controlled a legitimate business known as Concordia Developments Ltd. which had extensive mineral rights in South Africa. Concordia Developments Ltd. owned, among other properties, a perlite mine which is a commodity used in the building trade. The gang also organised an extraordinary racket in airline tickets which revealed the weaknesses of the system by which such tickets are sold through agents, sometimes being paid for, but at other times being merely debited. This kind of business was bound to lead to information in the hands of private persons which, if given to the police, would bring about the arrest and downfall of the gang. In order to prevent this, people who had such knowledge were lured by some specious bait into the Richardson premises where they were either tortured directly, usually by electric-shock treatment, or so terrified that they kept their mouths shut. Writing of this extraordinary affair some years ago, I described the outward respectability and the inner horror of the Richardson gang in these words:

'The ghastly violence that simmered under the surface was hidden by the business premises, the paraphernalia of files and telephones, the directorial desks, and the intensely respectable little detached houses (with garage) that Richardson and his men favoured as their private residences.'

The Richardson gang carried on their lucrative and sinister business for over three years before the police decided to act. There had been rumours reaching Scotland Yard before that and one or two complaints were made to local police stations. However, these stories appeared to the police to be so unlikely and indeed so bizarre that there was a reluctance to give them credibility. I think this was only natural. If one was told that what appeared to be a respectable business firm was using torture as a method of intimidation, one's natural reaction would be 'Nonsense. This kind of thing just does not happen in London. Besides, these people have a profitable legitimate business. Why should they turn to crime?'

. It was, of course, greed that induced Richardson to employ intimidation and torture. As soon as he became involved in illegal rackets that depended for their profitable continuation on no one going to the police and informing, the gang was committed to a policy of intimidation.

It may well have been the fact that Richardson employed Francis Fraser, who lived in Hove, that made it easy for Richardson to resort to torture, because Francis Fraser, who had a long history of sojourns in mental hospitals, was known as 'Mad Franky'. Mad Franky was a sadist and there was nothing he enjoyed more than being told by the boss to give the full treatment to anyone who had been lured into the Richardson office. Curiously enough, Mad Franky had survived for years without any psychiatric report being made upon him. He had been in prison, but no one had ever suggested that he was in any sense insane. However, he had this appetite for the infliction of pain and his manner when he was on a job was so menacing that the victims were often prepared to pay up before receiving the treatment. Mad Franky did not like this and usually managed to apply some torture in case they should forget their obligations as soon as they were out of the building.

The extraordinary danger to the public presented by the Richardson gang is shown clearly if we consider the amount of effort that was involved to arrest, prosecute and convict them. A party of detectives worked up to sixteen hours a day for nine months on the case. At every turn in their investigations the police came upon people who were terrified to speak. They were sure that if they did tell the police what they knew Richardson would learn of it and Mad Franky would knock at the door one night and carry out his diabolical business. Because of this the police had to provide protection for every single witness for the prosecution and even then the witnesses lived in a cold sweat of apprehension.

During the trial, which lasted for many weeks, attempts were made to intimidate the jurors. For instance, the mother of one of the jurors, who was seventy-five years of age, was told, 'You must see to it that the jury disagree.' In two other cases bribery was suspected. The jurors were never left alone for a single minute. They were watched over in court, escorted to and from their homes, constantly guarded even when they had to leave their houses for shopping. Richardson and most of his men might be in the dock, but they had friends outside who were willing to threaten and intimidate on their behalf. For a year after the case closed and Richardson and some other defendants were convicted, the police were still guarding the jurors whose verdict sent Richardson to prison. A friend who was present when Richardson was convicted and sentenced told me that he seemed to shake with inner anger when he heard the sentence. He glared at the jury and said, 'Thank you very much.' The words were uttered with such vindictive venom that the court was silenced by a chill of horror.

In addition to all this, Richardson and his gang had an elaborate police escort wherever they went. The police officers in charge of the case, Superintendent Victor Evans of Scotland Yard and Detective Superintendent Ronald Coles, were convinced that there was a very real danger of a rescue attempt by armed force and this they were determined should not happen. It was prevented if it was ever planned, but the incident shows the terrifying atmosphere of menace and violence that the gang were able to disseminate.

To go in detail into the evidence against Richardson and his gangsters would require a book in itself, and perhaps such a book should be written in the public interest to remind us how dangerous the organised criminal has now become, but in the confines of this chapter we cannot explore the weeks of evidence that were carefully and painfully built up. Sufficient it is to say that at the end of the long trial Mr. Justice Lawton, a tough, and good judge, sentenced Richardson to twenty-five years' imprisonment, saying:

'I am satisfied that over a period of years you were the leader of a large, disciplined, well-led and well-organised gang. One is ashamed to think one lives in a society which can produce men like you. By the sentence of this court, our society must show that it repudiates your criminal activities and is revolted by them. I have come to the conclusion that no penal system will cure you of crime. I hope that this heavy sentence will serve as an example to others who set themselves up as gang leaders and will show that they too will be struck down by the law.'

Then, most unusually, the judge ordered Richardson to pay up to two-thirds of the cost of the prosecution, the amount not to exceed twenty thousand pounds. The fact that Richardson was known to be able to raise such a sum of money shows the wealth that the gang were rapidly accumulating. Richardson's younger brother George, who was sentenced to ten years' imprisonment, was also ordered to pay twenty per cent of the cost of the prosecution, but in his case the sum was not to exceed two thousand pounds. The public and the press reacted favourably to these large fines. It had long been a criticism in Britain that the gangster, though losing his liberty if convicted, often enjoyed the fruits of his crime when he came out of prison.

Even with the fines imposed by the judge in addition to the prison sentences, it is thought that the public probably had to meet, through taxation, a sum approaching a quarter of a million pounds for this case alone. The total cost of the trial was believed to be one hundred and twenty-five thousand pounds and the cost of keeping the gang in prison for many years was going to amount to another fifty thousand pounds, while the losses directly due to the extortions of the gang ran into many thousands of pounds. So that the arrest, trial and conviction of the Richardson gang was a most expensive business. Certainly it was worth it, because the conviction of the Richardsons, taken together with the conviction of the Kray brothers, smashed the great gangs in London for the time being. It certainly did not kill them off for good. The current tendency is to concentrate on armed hold-ups, carried out by armed men with ruthless precision, and the conviction of these modern robbers has not yet been sufficiently certain or frequent to contain this dangerous development, made even more menacing by the fact that, in the absence of capital punishment, many gangsters carry guns as a matter of policy. Their reasoning is perfectly simple. If they are caught and convicted of armed robbery they are going to get a very long prison sentence in any case, and that sentence will not be greatly increased if they are convicted of murder. They are, therefore, prepared, if cornered, to shoot their way out. It is equally true to say that when capital punishment is operative the same gangsters, again as a matter of policy, do not carry fire-arms.

From time to time there is criticism of the newspapers, who are said to hamper the efforts of the police because of their natural desire to tell their readers everything at a time when the police wish to keep their investigations secret. However, it must be said that when the police do request the press to co-operate by not publishing all that they know, the press usually comply. They certainly did so in the terrible case we have been describing.

In fact, one newspaper, *The People,* gave the police vital help in arresting the Richardson gang. One of *The People* reporters, Roy East, had been offered three thousand pounds if he would turn over to the gang the information he had gathered about their activities. This was one of the cases in which the gang thought it more prudent to bribe than to torture. In fact, Mr. East handed his dossier over to Mr. Gerald McArthur, who supervised the whole elaborate police operation. Mr. Peter Brode, Assistant Commissioner for crime at Scotland Yard, thanked the paper for their public service.

He said: 'The Metropolitan Police are very grateful indeed for the help given by *The People* to the team of detectives whose work led to the Old Bailey sentences by Mr. Justice Lawton. I am personally aware of the help given to the police team by *The People* and I would like to express sincere thanks on behalf of the Metropolitan Police. Such help is extremely encouraging to the police.'

It is refreshing at a time when the police are being referred to as 'pigs' by a small, vociferous, demented section of society to realise that a great public newspaper took considerable trouble to further the cause of justice in this dangerous and notorious case, while their reporter turned down a sum of money which must have been extremely tempting and did not hesitate to do his duty as a member of the public.

We hope that the conviction of the Richardsons will mean London has been cleansed of torture for the time being.

The signs are that gang executions have not ceased and even in cases which were thought to be death by misadventure or suicide, such as the case of the respected ex-boxer Freddie Mills, it is now thought that the London underworld may well be responsible. The real danger arises out of the large sums of money which the gangsters now control. This money, often extorted from casinos, gambling joints and betting shops, is still not on a par with the huge fortunes of the American gangsters, but it is very considerable. In fact, it does not require a very large sum of money either to subvert the course of justice or to bribe many ordinary individuals. One thousand pounds in used bank notes is a great temptation to many men who may be earning between a thousand and two thousand pounds a year. The gangsters have such sums at their command. The whole aspect of the gangster has changed in Britain. He is no longer the hunted outlaw, living in and out of prison, often in dire poverty, shabbily dressed, hungry and disreputable. He often presents an appearance of respectability and affluence. Such a gangster has only to obtain the licence to operate a respectable gaming club and he is in a position to extend his criminal activities, secure behind his façade of legality. The new type of criminal often does not look like a criminal, live like a criminal or behave like a criminal. At first this change in the social strata of the gangsters tended to bewilder the police, who knew the old criminal class extremely well and certainly knew how to deal with them. They were reluctant to arrest men who appeared to be part of the well-to-do commercial pattern of the country. However, it has not taken the police long to re-orientate their ideas and, with a much better-educated police force, the police and the gangsters are now battling it out on an equal footing.

Although Richardson was fined in order to force him to make a contribution to the legal costs, his own defence was granted by the magistrate on legal aid, which means that the taxpayer may have to pay a bill of some fifteen thousand pounds. At the same time Richardson is said still to possess a South African mine worth at least a quarter of a million pounds. There is something very wrong here. The explanation is that the criminal and civil law of England did not walk hand in hand. Broadly speaking, criminal law in the past has been concerned solely with convicting persons charged with crime and sentencing them to death, to prison or to a period of probation. It has not been concerned with extracting compensation from the criminal. However, under the new laws the criminals can be forced to pay for their crimes or at least to help to pay for their crimes.

Looking back on the case of the Richardson gang, even so shortly after the trial, it seems almost incredible that, in fact, men whom the gang regarded as enemies or potential informers were lured to the Richardson premises and so terrified by pain or the threat of pain that they left as haunted, shaken and craven creatures who dared not go to the nearest police station which was just round the corner. It is a terrible warning that we must never allow torture to be used as an instrument of power by the criminals of this country. There are some people, very few, who can withstand torture, but most of us would do anything rather than be subjected to the systematic infliction of acute pain.

It is pleasant at a time when relations between the public and the police are not what they should be, and when the police are sometimes unjustly criticised and even reviled, to be able to say that, in this case, the force rendered the public a unique and outstanding service.

3

The Wrong Woman

ABDUCTION and holding to ransom, which goes by the popular name of kidnapping, is a crime that seldom if ever appears in the criminal calendar of assize court in Britain. Indeed, until December 29th, 1969, it seemed that kidnapping had virtually died out as a crime in Britain.

There were a number of reasons for this. The professional criminal class, who devote their whole time and energy to trying to make crime pay, were concentrating on massive and well-organised hold-ups. These enterprises were sometimes aimed at banks, but more often at money in transit, whether in the hands of security firms or in private hands. During 1968 and 1969 very large sums of money in used and untraceable bank notes were stolen in this way. Having established such a lucrative line of business, involved and dangerous crimes such as kidnapping just did not seem worth while. The public, too, had an abhorrence of kidnapping and all potential kidnappers knew that they would have the public ranged against them before they started. Then the crime of kidnapping itself if the aim is to extort money is a very difficult crime. The money has to be collected, usually from the relatives of the person kidnapped, and this presents all kinds of dangers to the conspirators.

The natural reaction of a family who have lost one of their members through a suspected kidnapping is immediately to inform the police. The police have an elaborate routine for dealing with the matter which includes a recording of every message received by the family, the tracing of fingerprints on any letters sent through the post, and various devices to lure the kidnappers into collecting the ransom money without actually receiving it, for instance a suitcase packed with what appears to be used and unmarked pound notes but which, in fact, only contains pound notes on the top layer, the rest of the bundle being paper cut to the exact dimensions of a pound note.

It is not too difficult, provided one has laid a good plan and knows the daily habits of a family, to seize the person perhaps of the wife who is known usually to be alone at certain hours. The absence of servants in most families these days makes the woman left alone while her husband goes to the office much more vulnerable than she would have been forty or fifty years ago. In kidnapping by definition we are only dealing with victims who are wealthy or thought by the kidnappers to be wealthy. The abduction of a woman if she is taken by surprise by two determined men is not too difficult. They can gag her and bind her or even put her to sleep and carry the body to the car waiting in the drive, or alternatively they can hold a gun at her head and say, 'Come with us.'

It is the ransom and its collection that makes kidnapping such a dangerous crime. No kidnapper has yet been able to devise a method of collecting ransom money without either incriminating himself or at least giving the police leads both as to his identity and the place from which he operates. Because of this kidnappers are very wary in collecting ransom and they usually threaten, often over the telephone, that any attempt to lay a police trap for them will result in the immediate death of the victim who is in their power. In spite of this, in most kidnappings the family and police co-operate and sometimes in the end the kidnappers, infuriated by the failure of their scheme, murder the victim.

The types of kidnapping we are discussing in this chapter are what you might call domestic kidnapping with the sole aim of extorting money, usually a very large sum of money. During the last three years an even more dangerous type of kidnapping has emerged, directed by the lunatic fringe of politics, people who have been perverted by the gibberish of Chairman Mao's little red book. These people would have been called anarchists in Edwardian times. They are now referred to as the Far Left. 'Political' kidnappings engineered by the anarchists always have one thing in common. They always seek to disguise their real aim, which is political chaos, by espousing or pretending to espouse a local cause. In Jordan this was the legitimate cause of the Arabs for the return of their homeland. In Quebec it was the not unnatural desire of a French-speaking province for greater autonomy. The political kidnappings are viler and more dangerous than the domestic kidnappings because their objective is usually different. As a rule they aim to release from prison sympathisers convicted of murder, sedition or riot. Although they may demand money this is not their prime objective and usually they are prepared to drop the demand for a ransom. This makes the political kidnapper much more difficult to arrest. He does not have to make that perilous contact to collect a suitcase full of money by which the domestic kidnapper runs a major risk of being trapped. In another chapter of this book I shall deal with the political kidnapper and will suggest that only the international imposition of the death penalty for all kidnappers is likely to reduce this savage and new development in the political and criminal age we appear to be entering.

On the 29th of December 1969 Mrs. Muriel McKay was snatched from her home in Wimbledon, so that when her husband Mr. Alick McKay returned from his office at *The News of the World* in Bouverie Street she had vanished. There were signs of a struggle, including overturned chairs and a telephone on the floor. Within a few hours the telephone rang in the McKay home and a voice demanded a million pounds for the ransom of Mrs. McKay, 'otherwise she will die'. It was obvious to the McKay family and to the police that a desperately serious situation had arisen. What the family did not know immediately was that Mrs. McKay had been kidnapped by mistake. Mr. Alick McKay was deputy chairman of *The News of the World* organisation. He and his wife were Australians, but had lived at St. Mary's House, Arthur Road, Wimbledon, for many years. The kidnappers had intended to seize the wife of Mr. Rupert Murdoch, the well-known Australian chairman of *The News of the World* organisation and a very wealthy man. This was the first extra-

ordinary aspect of this case. The second was that to this day
the body of Mrs. McKay has never been found. It was thought
at one time that without the production of the body a charge
of murder could not be brought against any accused, but, in
fact, this was not so. Of course, in most cases the body itself
is the most cogent evidence—the bullet wound in the head or
the arsenic in the stomach virtually prove that murder has
been done, though they do not prove or may not prove who
has done it.

The authorities seem to have been somewhat uneasy
concerning this aspect of the case and, to make quite certain
that the prosecution would be presented as effectively as
possible, Sir Peter Rawlinson, the Attorney General, led the
case for the Crown.

When they started their investigations the police had very
little to go upon, but one curious and significant incident had
taken place. On the 19th of December a man giving the name
of 'Shariff Mustapha' of Norbury Road, Streatham, called at
County Hall, saying that he had been involved in a minor car
accident. He said that his car had hit a Rolls-Royce and he
wanted the owner's address so that he could get in touch with
him. The man was given a form to fill up and the address
which the man received was the registered office of *The News
of the World* in Bouverie Street, which, of course, was an
address common to both Mr. Murdoch and Mr. McKay.

In December 1969 Mr. Murdoch and his wife were, in fact,
out of the country, but Mr. Murdoch's Rolls-Royce car made
a number of journeys between the office and St. Mary's
House, Wimbledon, so that if the kidnappers were trailing the
Rolls-Royce they would naturally assume that St. Mary's
House was the home of Mr. Murdoch. This probably accounts
for the tragic and ghastly error that resulted in the kidnapping
of Mrs. McKay.

At this point the police had in their possession the form
which 'Shariff Mustapha' had filled in in his attempt to get
the address of the owner of the Rolls-Royce. So there was
handwriting, apparently heavily disguised. Handwriting
experts are fallible, but at least they can usually tell with
certainty whether writing is normal and natural or disguised,

contrived and artificial. In this case they were quite certain
that the handwriting was disguised. Then why had the man
given the name 'Shariff Mustapha?' The spelling of the
second name was, to say the least, unusual. Was it perhaps not
his own name with which he would be familiar but a borrowed
name which he was not sure how to spell? So the police had a
case in which it appeared that a brown man or men, perhaps
Pakistanis or possibly Jamaicans, might be involved. Because
they believed that Mrs. McKay had probably been abducted
by two men they were on the trail of two dark members of
one of the foreign communities living in Britain.

As always in kidnapping cases where murder is feared, the
police questioned a very large number of people who might
know at least something about what was happening in
Wimbledon between four and six-thirty on the day of the
kidnapping. The net that they spread brought them in some
clues and for this they had to thank members of the public.
A Mr. Anderson, at twenty to five on the day of the kidnapping, was driving past Wimbledon Common towards
Putney. Ahead of him was a Volvo car, loitering or idling.
He decided to overtake it and, as he did so, he saw two men
inside, talking. The driver seemed to be about thirty-five
years old and the two men 'looked like Arabs'. Mr. Anderson
obviously was an observant person. About ten minutes later
Mr. Anderson was returning to Wimbledon in the opposite
direction and, rather to his surprise, he saw the Volvo again,
but this time it turned left into Church Road which leads to
St. Mary's Road. Mr. Anderson was certainly a useful
witness. And then just after six o'clock a woman was passing
the McKay house when she noticed that the lights were on,
the front door was shut and a dark-coloured saloon car was
parked in the drive.

Usually when she was alone in the house Mrs. McKay
kept the front door on a chain, but it is presumed that she
opened the door because her callers convinced her that they
had some legitimate reason for calling on her. It is possible
that they mentioned the matter of the accident, quoting the
number of the Rolls-Royce car, and such a corroborative
detail, combined with a plausible and smiling manner, might

have been enough to persuade Mr. McKay to open the door.

When Mr. Alick McKay arrived home in the chauffeur-driven Rolls-Royce he rang the doorbell but received no answer. He tried the handle and was surprised to find that the door opened. Something was wrong. He ran upstairs to look for his wife. She was not there. He tried to telephone to the police. The telephone line had been cut. About six hundred pounds worth of jewellery belonging to Mrs. McKay was also missing, as well as a reversible black and fawn coat which presumably she was wearing.

On the floor of the sitting room were spread out some copies of *The People* newspaper. One of these bore the whole palm-print of one of the kidnappers and this man's fingerprint also appeared on a letter written by Mrs. McKay, after she had been kidnapped, to her husband.

An elaborate kidnapping or murder hunt was then turned on by the police. Whether this was the right move at this particular juncture is at least debatable. It was hardly likely that Mrs. McKay would be murdered in this early stage even before a ransom had been demanded and it was most unlikely, in any event, that her body would be found anywhere near her home if the police were right in thinking that the dark-coloured saloon seen parked in front of the house by the woman witness was, in fact, the same car as had been observed by the interested Mr. Anderson.

However, the family did not have to wait long for the kidnappers to get in touch. Mr. McKay's daughter Diane and her husband David Dyer had driven in from Sussex to be with Mr. McKay so that he should have people around him in the house. When the telephone rang Mr. Dyer answered it because Mr. McKay, who had a weak heart, was in a prostrate condition from shock.

The message that David Dyer received over the telephone, in a voice that did not seem to be English but, in any case, appeared to be unnatural and disguised, was: 'Tell Mr. McKay it is M.3, the Mafia. We want a million pounds.'

The police decided, with the family, to offer a fake ransom in a suitcase and the Volvo car with its mysterious driver

driver passed the spot but did not fall into the trap. It was probably from that moment that Mrs. McKay was doomed. Eventually the police, sorting out a very large number of leads, closed in on lonely and isolated Rook's Farm, Stocking Pelham, Herts, which was the home of Arthur Hosein and Nizammodeen Hosein. They arrested the brothers and charged them with kidnapping and murder. For weeks after the arrest every foot of the thirty-acre smallholding, as well as much of the surrounding country, was searched for the body of Mrs. McKay. No body was found.

The trial before Mr. Justice Sebag Shaw ended in the conviction of both the brothers and their sentence to long terms of imprisonment. But the interest of this horrifying case is as acute today as it was when Mrs. McKay was abducted, for some extraordinary questions which in any ordinary kidnapping and murder case would have been answered in this strange case remain not only unanswered but a complete and baffling mystery.

Detective Chief Superintendent Wilfred Smith, as soon as the crime broke, set up a murder team with Detective Inspector John Minors and Detective Sergeant Jim Parker as his immediate lieutenants, who, in their turn, had a dozen other police officers and nearly a hundred constables engaged on the case. It was due to the painstaking perseverance of these policemen and the willing co-operation of the public that the Hosein brothers were eventually arrested and charged. All kinds of ploys were devised by the police to attempt to trap the kidnappers. For instance, Detective Sergeant Roger Street, who was about the same build and colouring as Ian McKay, Mr. McKay's son, was made up with his hair-styling and with his hair dyed exactly the same colour, wearing some of his clothes and his glasses. Sergeant Street then carried the ransom to the destination. However, nearly fifty policemen, mainly detectives, who were armed, surrounded the spot at a distance with instructions that if the kidnapper appeared with Mrs. McKay they were to rush the kidnapper and rescue Mrs. McKay. Many more police-men, posing as members of the public, used another fifty cars to motor along roads adjacent to the ransom spot. The police even had the idea of dressing up five or six of their young men as Hell's Angels, wearing leather coats and helmets duly emblazoned with swastikas or Hell's Angels symbols. This particular idea, though brilliant enough, may have had something to do with the fact that the kidnappers were frightened away. The young policemen, although dressed as Hell's Angels, drove their motorcycles in an upright position their broad shoulders painfully suggesting that they were men accustomed to discipline. They also made all the correct traffic signals, scrupulously observing the Highway Code. In short, they were dressed as Hell's Angels but they did not behave in the least like these rampaging thugs of the road.

The police used new, scientific and highly sophisticated methods to identify the voices in the various conversations that took place, both at the McKays' house and in various telephone kiosks. The voice is first recorded and this recording is played through electronic equipment which gives a graph that varies according to the inflexions, the emphasis and the timbre of the voice. How reliable this may be has not yet been proved, but it probably is a valuable aid to police investigation. In any case, both the family and the police were convinced that the voices of the kidnappers were Pakistani or West Indian.

The unanswered questions in the trial, which in spite of the arrest and convictions of the murderers are still being made the subject of investigation, are these:

There is no direct evidence that Mrs. McKay was taken immediately to Rook's Farm or indeed that she was ever taken to Rook's Farm where the Hosein brothers lived. Was she taken to some other house, for instance, in Streatham where there is a very large West Indian community? Who actually killed her and how was she killed? The Hosein brothers have been convicted of the crime but did they both do it or did one of them do it or perhaps did a third party commit the murder? These questions have never been conclusively answered. Finally, how was the body disposed of? It is comparatively easy if one has the time to burn flesh, though it makes a ghastly smell. But bones are not

C

easily disposed of. Again, is Mrs. McKay's body perhaps walled up in the cellar of some house in a part of London where the Hoseins had friends? I must confess that I find the fact that these questions are unanswered highly disturbing and it is strange that the first police reaction was that it was doubtful whether Mrs. McKay had been kidnapped at all. The trial at least answered that question. She was certainly kidnapped.

The judge was generous in his praise of the police and the way they tackled a difficult and dangerous case. But, as it turned out (and it is so easy to be wise after the event), was the case really a dangerous one? The Hoseins could have been armed but it was extremely unlikely. Was the very elaborate police operation which surrounded the offer of a purported ransom in a country lane at High Cross, not far from Ware in Hertfordshire, not in itself calculated to deter the highly suspicious and nervous kidnappers? Would not one man, driven in the McKay car by the actual chauffeur, carrying a single automatic revolver, have been enough? As it was, the whole countryside around for miles was teeming with police disguised as commercial travellers or survey men on the roads or Hell's Angels. I would have thought that the operation was on far too grand a scale and almost calculated to defeat itself by scaring the kidnappers.

One speculates as to the priorities which the police have when they are faced with a case of this kind. In fact, the kidnapping is a very secondary importance. It is the killing of the victim that is of paramount importance. This has to be prevented at all costs, so that whatever operations in regard to the ransom the police decide upon it must look from the point of view of the kidnappers as if the family had decided to go it alone and had refused to co-operate with the police, fearing that the threat of murder would be carried out. If this had been done then the roads around the ransom spot would have been much more deserted and, in any case, only genuine members of the public would have been using them. It is dangerous to send a single detective with the ransom money to the ransom spot, but it may be the only way. The trailing of the kidnappers if they can be persuaded to pick up the ransom is, of course, an operation of the utmost difficulty. But, as this operation was clearly being done by motor car one would have thought that it would have been possible to have blocked the few roads that led from the ransom spot after the kidnappers had approached the district.

The police search of Rook's Farm and the entire neighbourhood could not have been more thorough. Floors and drains were taken up. A deep well was emptied and searched. Ponds were drained, hedges were cut and earth was turned over. The result was absolutely nothing. The weather was freezing at the time and the search was hampered by snow as well. But the final result of this unique case, which must surely take its place as one of the most bizarre in the annals of crime, is that two men have been convicted of a kidnapping and a murder which we still do not know the location of or the method by which it was effected. And we still do not know where the body of Mrs. McKay rests or by what awful means it was consumed.

The police apparently are convinced that all the questions will one day be answered, for here they have on their file a murder case which has been completed but a case in which at least three of the basic questions have not been answered. This is a situation that I believe has never occurred before in the history of English murder.

There is one other major question which has been officially answered but which one may doubt whether it has been answered correctly. Certainly there was the most strong circumstantial evidence on which the Hosein brothers could be convicted of the abduction, but was there that conclusive evidence 'beyond all reasonable doubt' to convict them of Mrs. McKay's murder? Was not the court in fact saying: 'These men kidnapped Mrs. McKay. They had her in their possession and now she has disappeared, so they must have murdered her.' There seems to me to be a *non sequitor* here. Does it really follow conclusively, or at all, that the kidnappers must have been the murderers? Was there not a reasonable doubt as to this, even taking into account the incriminating and contradictory statements by which the brothers themselves made it possible for the court to return a verdict of guilty?

While everyone must share the terrible bereavement of the family, and admire the immense effort the police put into this case, still there remains doubt and disquiet with so many vital questions remaining unanswered. If, as the police hope, some day the fog will clear and the questions can be answered, those who are troubled, as I am, by this terrible and mystifying crime will at least be relieved.

If it is true that murder will out, then we shall know how Mrs. McKay met her death. Until then we must remain mystified and puzzled.

4

Political Intimidation à la Mode

MR. ENOCH POWELL, the well-known prophet of the Tory Party and possibly its future leader, whose ideas on Britain's role in the world I profoundly disagree with, is right about two matters, and one of these is his conviction that the outbreak of spasmodic street revolution in most countries and the adoption of new techniques of intimidation, is not an accident but a carefully planned design of destruction originated and executed by the highest echelons of the Communist Party.

We should pay attention to what Mr. Powell says about such matters because he is virtually the only political figure of stature in Britain speaking his mind on this important question and his words do not merely have a local significance. He is reported in the press in Europe, in North America and in the Spanish and Portuguese languages press of South America. There is, I think, a general feeling among the British public that Mr. Heath is a decent, dedicated and hard-working public servant but that he lacks the indefinable quality of leadership—and one must have some misgivings about a British Prime Minister who finds it necessary to employ, at a reputed fourteen thousand pounds a year, a distinguished Jewish gentleman as a think-tank. Such a situation surely leaves the way open to the more concrete and dynamic personality of Mr. Powell.

However this may be, revolution is on the march. What is entirely new are the techniques which the very small minority concerned have adopted. In another chapter of this book we examine the enormous sky-jack operation put on by people calling themselves the Front for the Liberation of Palestine.

In this chapter we examine the new political technique of abduction or kidnapping which frequently leads to the murder of the victim. This is an atrocious development and universal capital punishment for this crime is probably the only measure which will effectively stamp it out.

One of the most daring and diabolical examples of the kidnap technique occurred during August 1970 in Montevideo, the capital of Uruguay, and here I would like to quote the *Daily Telegraph* report on this matter, because it does show cool, factual British reporting at its very best. Although the subject is charged with dynamite and emotive to a degree, the report sticks to the facts virtually without comment, allowing the reader to form his own judgment on what has occurred. It is this kind of reporting that makes us see how valuable an asset to a nation is the freedom of the press.

In their issue of Wednesday, 12th August, the *Telegraph* reported the extraordinary sequence of events in these words:

'Police and thousands of Army troops sealed off Montevideo from the rest of Uruguay yesterday and made a door-to-door search for an American scientist and a Brazilian diplomat threatened with execution by the Left-wing Tupamaros guerillas holding them hostage.

'Authorities raided a suspected Tupamaros camp on the outskirts of the capital, making four arrests and confiscating revolvers, hand grenades, machine-guns and explosives. But they found no trace of the two men, despite telephone calls claiming that the Brazilian had been killed.

'Mr. Dan Mitrione, 50, an American security adviser, was killed on Monday and the guerillas said the two other hostages would be shot unless the Uruguayan Government freed 150 political prisoners.

'The Government has refused to deal with the kidnappers.

'Congress has given President Jorge Pacheco Areco power to suspend constitutional rights in the search for the two men. They are Mr. Claude Fly, 65, employed by the Uruguay Ministry of Agriculture, and Senhor Aloysio Gomide, 41, First Secretary and Consul of Brazil.

'The Government is empowered to search homes without

warrants, seize property of prisoners, ignore habeas corpus appeals, use secret instead of public accusations, open mail, limit freedom to enter and leave the country, prohibit meetings, and curtail freedom of speech and of the Press.

'Military trucks and police cars made surprise dawn raids and there were a number of arrests of suspected terrorists. Police said those held included Andres Cultelli Chiribao, 48, a suspected Tupamaro senior officer.

'Meanwhile the Brazilian Foreign Minister, Senhor Mario Gibson Barbosa, sent a sharply-worded Note to his Uruguayan counterpart, Jorge Periano Facio, calling on the Uruguayan Government to do everything in its power to obtain Gomide's freedom.

'"In view of the barbarous, cold and premeditated crime committed by the terrorists who assassinated Mr. Mitrione, the danger is growing that Consul Aloysio Gomide will be similarly assassinated," Senhor Barbosa said.

'The Brazilian Government confirmed it has put Brazilian troops "on the alert" along the Uruguay–Brazil border to watch for Tupamaros trying to flee north into Brazil.

'But officials in Brasilia declined to comment on a report by the *Jornal do Brazil* in Rio de Janeiro that eight planeloads of paratroopers had been flown to Santana do Livramento, the Brazilian town separated from the Uruguayan city of Rivera by only one street.'

The report shows very clearly that once this method of abduction and murder is adopted all kinds of dangers arise. There is the danger that the authorities, infuriated by the secret menace in their midst, may hit back at the murderers with unjustified arrests and with torture. There is the danger of war between the country in which the abduction has taken place and the country whose national is being victimised. There is, of course, the immediate danger that diplomatic relations between the two countries will be broken off and that, as a result of this, their trade will suffer, which in itself will affect the lives of millions of ordinary citizens not in any way involved either in the crime or in its detection and suppression. So political kidnapping reveals itself as a vile and dangerous criminal act.

I think I should make it clear here that there is no difference whatever in the eyes of the law, or for that matter, as far as I know, in the eyes of God, between the man who murders from a political motive and the man who poisons his father in order to inherit his money prematurely. There is an unfortunate inclination on the part of the public to distinguish between the two and perhaps this is aided and abetted by the use of the word assassination to describe political murders whereas domestic murders are usually described as 'killings'. In fact the blunt use of the term murder to describe a murder appears to be becoming unfashionable. The public in many countries, and especially perhaps in the United States and in Britain, are being conditioned into believing that every killing has its justifiable excuse. In the case of the domestic murderer he is obviously a deranged person. His mind is not normal. He does not distinguish clearly between right and wrong and therefore should not be held responsible for his actions, far less hang by the neck until he is dead. In the case of the political murderer he, of course, is something of a hero. His real aim is to substitute a communist type of government for the existing establishment he dislikes. He wishes to introduce the well-known liberty of the person, freedom of faith and freedom of speech which are such a marked aspect of the Russian and Chinese regimes. To convict and execute such a hero because he has put someone to death is, we are told, most unreasonable and reactionary. Revolution is always accompanied by bloodshed anyway, and it is natural and proper for revolutionaries to murder people. I hope I have made my point.

Let us pass now to the Canadian example of political abduction. Considering that the vast area of Canada has so recently been inhabited and made subject to law and order, it is little less than astounding how law-abiding the Canadians are. They are a people with a deep love of freedom and, as a rule, they grudge their authorities any special powers. The forces of law and order, typified by the Canadian Mounted Police, have a long tradition of 'getting their man'. Although Canada has struck out on her own to some extent away from the British tradition in which she was nurtured, this great country does retain an intense respect for law and law enforcement and for complete equality before the law which originally they derived from the British heritage. It is all the more surprising, therefore, when we find one of the most flagrant examples of political kidnapping taking place in a Canadian province and leading to murder.

In spite of the looming possibility of Britain 'entering' Europe, the English are still a very insular people and the majority are ill-informed of what goes on abroad. For instance, if you were to question fifty citizens on the streets of London as to what they knew of the province of Quebec in Canada you would not, believe me, receive an accurate and comprehensive description of Quebec.

First of all, it is an enormous province with an area of over half a million square miles, much bigger than most European countries. It has a tradition and a history entirely its own arising from the defeat of French ambitions in Canada by the armed forces of Britain. The total population is nearly five million, of which nearly four million are of French descent and most of these are French-speaking. Less than three-quarters of a million are of British descent. There are some fifteen thousand citizens of Indian origin. Virtually the whole of the population of British descent is concentrated in Montreal which has a population of over a million. This British population controls a great deal of the business and finance of the province, not because providence gave them positions of privilege but because during the last fifty years they have shown greater expertise in these fields than the French-Canadians and have been prepared to work harder.

The city of Quebec itself, which has a population of under a quarter of a million, is predominantly French in origin. Quebec is the provincial capital. The Legislative Council members, twenty-four in number, are appointed for life by the Lieutenant-Governor. The ninety-two members of the Legislative Assembly are elected. Representation of the province at Ottowa, the national capital, is by twenty-four senators and seventy-three members of the House of Commons.

Quebec has always been the central hope of the French-Canadians in their aspirations for independence. The city was founded in 1608 as a purely French colony and until 1763 it was the base from which French nationalism in Canada operated. In 1763 the French empire in North America collapsed and Quebec was ceded to Britain. Most of the high officials of the Quebec Government returned to France and this has tended to leave in the hands of the Catholic priests some of the political leadership of Quebec, at least until very recent times. The Quebec Act of 1774 guaranteed the rights of its own law and religion to the Province of Quebec and the people of Quebec have always guarded their special position with zeal and determination. For instance, in the war of 1939–45 French-Canadian public opinion was so strong that it forced the Government of Canada into refusing to adopt conscription for the overseas service of the army. Finally, the French-Canadians breed freely and this accentuates rather than mitigates the problems of the Quebec cuckoo in the Canadian nest.

It is necessary to bear in mind this simple outline so that we can put the shocking events that occurred in Quebec during October 1970 into perspective.

Members of the Quebec Liberation Front, determined to step up the agitation for a free Quebec which General de Gaulle, in one of his sillier and less scrupulous moments, had endorsed, kidnapped Mr. Pierre Laporte, Quebec's Minister of Labour, and a little later they kidnapped Mr. James Cross, who was the British Trade Commissioner, and held them to ransom. The rebels demanded a large sum of money, presumably to finance their rebellion, free transportation out of the country for the kidnapppers, and the publication in the news media of the province of their political manifesto. Only the last demand was met. For the the rest, the Government of Canada, under the premiership of Mr. Trudeau, himself a French-Canadian, remained remarkably strong and firm. They made it abundantly clear that they would not capitulate to terror and that intimidation, as far as they were concerned, would get nowhere.

The F.L.Q. (it was inevitable that the name should be

abbreviated) had a special grudge against Mr. Laporte because in his earlier political career he had appeared to support most of the aims of the French-speaking nationalists. But in recent years he had become disillusioned with the extremists and had given his powerful support to the axiom of one Canada, united and indivisible.

On Saturday, 17th October, Mr. Laporte was found murdered, his body in the boot of a green Chevrolet, the same car in which he was kidnapped, parked near Montreal's St. Hubert airport. Mr Laporte, who was forty-nine, and had a wife and two children, had been shot through the head. His wrists had been slashed and he had apparently bled to death, possibly being finished off by the gun to make certain that no life remained. This act of horror outraged and deeply shocked the Canadian people and they rallied behind Mr. Trudeau in the steps that he was prepared to take. Parliament gave him special powers of arrest and detention and of search to enable him to have a free hand.

The Federal Parliament heard of the murder in the midst of a thirteen-hour emergency session. A great crowd gathered outside the Parliament building. The general reaction of the public was 'Oh God, what has happened to Canada?' All flags were lowered to half-mast and the TV and radio stations played funeral music.

Mr. Pierre Trudeau described the murder as a dastardly assassination by a band of murderers, a cruel and senseless act conceived in cold blood. Mr. John Diefenbaker, a former Premier, described the murder as a diabolical act of savagery. Mr. Real Caouette, leader of Canada's Social Credit Party, went further. He said that the leaders of the F.L.Q. should be put before a firing squad immediately, while Mr. Peter Knowles of the Democratic Party said: 'These are the kind of people we have never had in Canada before.' Two young men were arrested and charged with the kidnapping.

At the same time that all this was going on, extraordinary measures were being taken to save the life, if that was possible, of Mr. Cross, the kidnapped British diplomat. The Government of Canada was willing, if Mr. Cross was returned alive and well, to fly the murderers to any country that would welcome them—possibly Algeria or Cuba. To implement this project the government declared the Concordia Bridge, spanning two islands in the St. Lawrence river at Montreal, Cuban territory where the kidnappers could hand over Mr. Cross with a guarantee of immunity from arrest, after which a government plane would fly them to Cuba.

There is no doubt that the murderers were encouraged by the fact that in 1967 capital punishment had been abolished on an experimental five-year basis except for the murder of a policeman or a head of state. The result of this was, of course, that the murderers, even if they were caught, could only be sentenced to imprisonment for a long period which they would hope might be greatly reduced if Quebec nationalism were to win the day in Canada.

Every kind of confusion and hazard surrounded the subterranean negotiations between the authorities and the kidnappers. For instance, the boot of the car that contained the corpse of Mr. Laporte was not opened for five hours because the police suspected a booby trap, which was another device which had already been employed on several occasions by the evil men of the F.L.Q.

The Canadian Broadcasting Corporation's radio and television stations interrupted their programmes to announce that both Mr. Laporte and Mr. Cross had been executed, but after Mr. Laporte's body was found the police withdrew their statement that Mr. Cross was dead.

I was lucky enough to see a B.B.C. Panorama special programme which featured Mr. Lester Pearson, former Canadian Prime Minister, speaking on the progress towards equality for French-Canadians. Perhaps the use of that phrase is misleading because, of course, French-Canadians are completely equal under the law with British Canadians. They enjoy all the old rights of freedom together. Mr. Lester Pearson said that progress towards equality was never fast enough for a few extremists, the terrorist fringes. He pointed out that wonderful progress was being made and that the problem, almost for the first time in Canadian history, was being pursued in an active way. However, to an outsider it would seem that the 'problem' is an extremely difficult one

The sense of frustration and inferiority that French-Canadians are said to feel has its roots in the domination of the national business economy by British Canadians. French-Canadians feel that the great employers of labour—mainly British by descent—discriminate against French-Canadians when jobs become available. One of the reasons for this is that many, if not most, French-Canadians insist on speaking French, whereas English is the national language of Canada and in a very special sense the commercial and industrial language of Canada. The result of all this is that the abduction and murder is set in a very political frame that does not have its exact counterpart in any other country.

Of course, the Canadian Government has been criticised for their conduct of the whole affair. There were those who said that the demands of the kidnappers should have been met immediately, it being the duty of the government to save the lives of the Minister, Mr. Laporte, and the diplomat, Mr. Cross, at all cost. This obligation, the critics said, was an absolute priority. But I think that moderate opinion everywhere will feel that the Canadian Government faced the crises with great courage.

A huge army and police hunt for the murderers was mounted in Quebec and throughout Canada and even in the United States, where it was thought that some of the guilty men had fled over the border into that country. On direct orders from the Prime Minister all members of the government were specially guarded and all government buildings likewise had their military guard. An incredible situation had arisen. A very small number of men, perhaps not more than a hundred in all, had been able to hold a great nation to ransom. The threat was there for all to see.

The whole tense and dramatic incident was made even more strained by the desperate pleas of the captured men to the authorities. For instance, a note was found in a litter basket in a Montreal square after a tip-off from the terrorists. Dated 7 a.m. on the Sunday, it was from Mr. Laporte to his wife and was described by the police as genuine. It read as follows:

'Darling, I am well and in good health and have passed a good night.

'I insist that you and the children take things in such a fashion as not to endanger your health. The important thing is for the authorities to move quickly. My love to everybody.

'Pierre'

One of the French-speaking radio stations quoted a letter alleged to be from Mr. Laporte warning that there would be three more kidnappings if the ransom demands were not met, and in a letter addressed to the Premier of Quebec, Mr. Bourassa, Mr. Laporte wrote:

'Please act quickly and avoid a blood bath. It is my life or death. I count on you.'

Perhaps nothing shows the cruelty of the kidnappers and the whole desperate situation as clearly as these notes from the doomed man only hours before his death. He knew what was coming and in language that had to be restrained he pleaded with the authorities to obtain his release.

In the case of Mr. Cross the firm stand of the Canadian Government paid off. The kidnap hideaway house was surrounded by a ring of armed police and soldiery. The kidnappers turned craven and surrendered on a promise (which was carried out) to fly them to Cuba, where they got a somewhat cool reception. The Concordia Bridge idea— making a Canadian bridge temporary Cuban territory— proved practical and effective.

Mr. Cross, after weeks in the direst peril, was released and free. He flew back to Britain. In accordance with Civil Service rules he was not permitted to write the story which the whole free world would have liked to hear, the terrible suspense story of his captivity.

It is, however, a sombre reflection that the men responsible were neither sentenced to life imprisonment nor hanged. I have not noticed that those who have written on these incidents have made any comment on the sinister fact that political abductors, by the nature of their crime, are in a much better position than other thugs who are captured for crimes no graver and often less dangerous.

The challenge of the kidnap murderer does not only exist in Uruguay and in the Province of Quebec in Canada. The same technique is being adopted in other countries where similar organisations exist. It is no use pretending any more that this pattern of political piracy is spontaneous or that it is dedicated to some moral political motive. When it comes down to brass tacks we always find that the murderers have links with the communist world. If they escape or are deported they always wish to be deported to the Soviet Union, to China, or to some satellite country with which they have good relations, and if we read with care and understanding what the communists themselves have said concerning their aims, right back to Karl Marx and right up to today, the link becomes completely understandable. The communists have always disdained to cover up their basic ambition of world conquest. It may pay them from time to time to cloak their overall design in such protection as is afforded by a local 'liberation' movement. This does not make the slightest difference to their real objective.

That great objective can be broken down into several channels. Perhaps the first is to gain military control of more territory and more ocean area year by year. The second objective is to capture the hearts and minds of a majority of the public in each country outside the large section of the world they already control by an apparatus of fear and force such as has not been witnessed since the heyday of the Third Reich. This objective is pursued mainly through the news media. The third objective is to disrupt the West by constant industrial strike action. The fourth objective is to capture and manipulate the student bodies in all countries and to dedicate the students to revolution; and, finally, the fifth objective is to employ new techniques of intimidation, such as kidnapping and murder which we have described in this chapter, in order to weaken and eventually to replace established authority.

Everyone knows that there are injustices in the world and that a great deal needs to be done to remedy those injustices, but our democratic process, which we did not easily win, was designed for the sole purpose of securing progress with freedom but without bloodshed. It is this peaceful evolutionary democratic progress which is now being challenged by a gun held at its head.

In this context the Quebec kidnappings have a world significance, and in five years' time, when we may have to decide whether to capitulate or to fight revolution of this type, we may look back with gratitude to the stand made by the Government of Canada.

5

Prince Hari Singh and Mr. Robinson

I DO not know if Indian maharajahs have come your way so that you already know the diverse influences that tended to create a race of men unique in the world long after their natural period had passed?

If you have never known a maharajah, as it were, in full regalia in India, or perhaps staying with his A.D.C. and retainers at the Savoy Hotel, London, or even if you do know the background of royal India, the following introduction to the extraordinary case of Prince Hari Singh and Mr. and Mrs. Robinson may be of interest to you.

With the break up of the Mogul empire early in the eighteenth century a number of princely rulers were left in control of vast territories in the Indian sub-continent. Before the British arrived they were apt to go to war with one another or to practise power politics and diplomacy in a tradition of what we may call honourable treachery. Their rivalries were intense and their ambition was unlimited.

For our purpose it is, I think, important to realise the kind of men they were. They were brought up from childhood as being semi-divine. They were told that their people did not have any 'rights', but at the same time their people could petition them and could supplicate the court if they wished action to be taken in any particular matter. They were taught only to marry into their own families or the family of a neighbouring state of equal power and prestige. They believed that they had the right to add any woman they desired to their harem. They expected and obtained the most profound respect from all their subjects, including any ministers of state whom they might from time to time

D

employ. It was traditional that all power, all laws, all regulations, emanated from the ruler, who had the right to put his subjects to death if they displeased him. Naturally if a subject was thought to be plotting against the throne, or to be in the pay of a rival prince, he was tortured until he confessed, after which he was usually put to death—slowly.

To us in our enlightened, compassionate, computerised wisdom this outlook on life seems to belong to another world. Today we only kill innocent civilians and burn children alive when our ideological principles are outraged, or our financial world interests are threatened. However this may be, the concept of absolute monarchy as it existed in India did produce a very special kind of man and the realisation of this fact makes the case of Hari Singh more interesting and more peculiar.

I have indicated that when the great Mogul empire, which rivalled the Chinese empire at Pekin, broke up, the princes of India, though numerous and powerful, were a chaotic body because of their constant feuding and private wars. Then at the end of the eighteenth century came the British, first as a trading company with forts at Madras, Calcutta and Bombay, then as a company with many attributes of sovereignty, and finally as the British Government of India, a situation that received its final accolade and sanction when Queen Victoria became Empress of India.

Now the coming of the British presented the princes with what these days (as Mr. Macmillan has pointed out) we wrongly call a problem. What we mean, of course, is a difficult situation. The princes, in spite of their elevated and almost god-like position, had all the natural patriotism and dislike of foreigners which was shared by the Indian masses. Of course, with over four hundred Indian rulers including the lesser rajahs, there were princes of every kind, princes arrogant, princes benign, princes devout, princes scandalous and princes who, in spite of their upbringing, contrived to maintain a balanced and moderate attitude towards life, and even towards their own subjects. But one and all resented the assumption of sovereign power in India by a foreign hierarchy whose speech, religion and way of life were entirely different from their own.

The first reaction of the princes to the rapidly encroaching tide of British power was to intrigue against it. And occasionally to fight against it with valour in the old tradition. At first it seemed uncertain whether the real enemy was going to be the British or the French, but it soon became clear that the British were tougher and more ruthless and better organised, so it was the British with whom the princes would have to deal. The princes of India, as a whole, prided themselves on being masters of diplomacy as well as of war and if diplomacy necessitated a certain amount of subterfuge and chicanery, then they were masters of these arts as well.

To their intense surprise, over the years, the British discovered that in this early period of their association with India, long before the advent of the British Indian Civil Service, they were at least as cunning as their adversaries. If a maharajah forged a treaty to enhance his position, the British would promptly produce an equally forged treaty bearing a date before that of the prince's document. If the maharajahs believed that their intelligence concerning what the British intended to do next was excellent, they discovered that their own secret plans were almost invariably known to the British before they could be executed.

It was not the Christian morality or the democratic principles of the British that impressed the princes. It was the native cunning of the British leaders backed by the armed discipline of British troops who did not waver under attack and who, on the whole, were a match for greatly superior levies of royal troops.

In these circumstances, without consulting each other, but by an almost unanimous urge, the princes decided to do a deal, first with the company and then with the British Government. The details of this deal were infinitely varied because the circumstances, the prestige, the power and the territories of each maharajah were different. But by and large the deal amounted to this: We, the British sovereign power, will sign treaties with you, the princes of India, whereby you will be left as maharajahs or as rajahs in control of your traditional lands and subjects, in return for which you will indicate a token allegiance to the overall authority of the British Government. We will leave you undisturbed to rule your people provided you do not murder and torture them, in which case we may, most regrettably, have to remove the guilty prince and place another member of the family upon the throne. All your revenues and palaces will remain yours and when you go abroad appropriate honour will be paid to you as sovereign rulers of your respective kingdoms.

The princes did not like the deal at first, but as time went on, and the British became omnipotent, they realised that it was the kind of deal that they probably would not receive from any other conqueror. It was inspired by the intense respect which the British had for monarchy and monarchical institutions. Moreover, as the rights of the princes were embodied in a treaty which appeared to be signed by two independent sovereign parties, and as the language of the treaties was most carefully chosen to conceal any element of *force majeur*, the pride of the princes was saved while their vital interests were protected.

As it turned out, the great deal had considerable advantage for the princes themselves. They could not go to war with each other any more and this made life much less hazardous and exhausting. They found that the upper echelons of British rule were represented by men with an intense respect for princely rank and a nice sensitivity to protocol. The British Indian Government, too, brought into the affair a sense of order that the princely hierarchy had hitherto lacked. This was achieved largely by the system of gun salutes. The greatest maharajahs, such as Hyderabad, Kashmir and Gwalia, were entitled to twenty-two gun salutes, lesser maharajahs to eighteen, and so on down the scale until minor rulers were only able to evoke twelve roars from the ceremonial cannons. This new order of affairs pleased the princes, especially those entitled to the maximum honour.

Over a century, approximately the whole of the nineteenth century, the relationship between the Indian princes and the

British Government settled down into a well-established groove. The only thing that was lacking was the presence of supreme white majesty in India. Queen Victoria took the conservative view that she did not have to travel abroad except occasionally to visit relatives in Europe, because it was suitable that all her subjects, including two hundred and fifty million Indian subjects, should come and see her wherever she might be, at Windsor, Sandringham or Balmoral. However, she did make some concessions. For instance, she had a very picturesque guard of Indian officers for great occasions. Her son, Edward VII, never got round to going to India although he was Emperor of India. He was too busy promoting the *Entente Cordiale* with France, winning the Derby, and caring for a number of favourite ladies who were fortunate enough to win his appreciative protection. It was left to his son, the sailor, George V, to go to India and to preside over one of the most magnificent scenes which the world had ever witnessed, the Delhi Durbar of 1911. The object of this Durbar was for the rulers of India to meet their emperor and for the emperor to meet the maharajahs, but there was also a little matter of allegiance and salutation. While the King-Emperor sat in gilded glory, the maharajahs, in strict order of precedence, approached him, salaamed, and took up their position to the right or to the left of the throne. As each prince brought with him a great retinue of queens, concubines, elephants, retainers and servants, the Delhi Durbar was probably the greatest show on earth.

Curiously enough, there was not another Durbar on this scale until Lord Mountbatten, as Viceroy, was saying the British goodbye to India. He organised one last splendid splash of regal magnificence, but it was a sad occasion, for, in spite of the protestations of friendship, everyone knew that the treaties were dead, that Britiain, after a hundred and fifty years of dominion, was quitting. Everyone knew that from now on the golden children of Indian royalty were on their own and would have to cope, as best they could, with a new, nationalist democratic government which did not share the sentiments which had made the British Government partners of the maharajahs in India.

I hope this introduction to the royal scene in India has not bored you. Just as the connoisseur appreciates a good wine more because he knows its birthplace, its environment and its traditional qualities, so it may be that this sketch of the world of the Indian maharajahs will enable us to understand the strange case of Prince Hari Singh, the nephew and heir presumptive of the Maharajah of Kashmir, who later, when he came to the throne himself, was known as General His Highness Shri Maharajah Hari Singh Bahadur, Indar-Mahindar, Supar-i-Saltanat-i-Inglishia, G.C.S.I., G.C.V.O., G.C.I.E., the Maharajah of Jammu and Kashmir.

The whole panorama of events connected with the attempt to intimidate and to blackmail Hari Singh which resulted in a long, civil case, followed by separate criminal proceedings, the employment of a veritable host of legal talent and a number one story for the European and American press, was cleverly contrived.

With the ending of the first world war in 1918, everyone, except the widows and relatives of the million dead, wanted to forget the carnage, the horror and the deprivations of war. It was a time to celebrate. It was a time to forget, it was a time to drown the nightmare and to dream a new dream. As part of this somewhat hectic social reaction a Victory Ball was organised at the Albert Hall in London on the 11th November, which, at that time and for many years thereafter, was observed as Armistice Day.

The Albert Hall is a wonderful building with tiers and tiers of boxes, a great stage and a vast auditorium. When it is full it generates an atmosphere unmatched anywhere else in London. On the night we are speaking of it was full to overflowing for a great spectacle and a great ball. The proceedings started before midnight and went on till the morning. Everyone who came to the ball, or nearly everyone, was fortified with celebratory champagne. Nearly all the most beautiful young women of London were there, squired by the young men who had been lucky enough to come home alive. In a box on the first row was a very gay party which included a Mrs. Robinson and a close woman friend. In the next box, as it happened, was the man whom the British public were to know as 'Mr. A.', the Prince Hari Singh, and his A.D.C., Major Maboob.

Florence Maud Robinson was married to Charles Ernest Robinson, who was a very curious character. The police had a file on him because of his association with con men and tricksters, but they had never been able to pin anything on Mr. Robinson since he had emigrated from Australia to settle in England.

Now, although the juxtoposition of the box of Prince Hari Singh and that of Mrs. Robinson appeared to be accidental, there is some reason to believe that in fact the matter was pre-arranged. The prince, in addition to Major Maboob, had an English aide-de-camp, Captain Charles Arthur, and he had around him also a Mr. Montagu Noel Newton who acted in the capacity which we should now describe as being that of his public relations consultant. Mr. Newton actually had been to prison because he had impersonated Lewis and Lewis, the most fashionable and well-known solicitors of the day.

Champagne and lobster were served in the boxes and no doubt the effervescent gaiety of the music and the dancers also had its effect on everyone. Prince Hari Singh noticed Mrs. Robinson and Mrs. Robinson noticed Prince Hari Singh. They met that night, and frequently in the weeks that followed. Mrs. Robinson rented a house in Mayfair to make this more convenient for the prince and by the greatest good fortune Major Maboob, bless his loyal heart, formed an affection for her woman friend, so everyone was happy. It seems that Mrs. Robinson was completely captivated by Hari Singh. He was a manly, generous person and, of course, he had around him the glamour of regality. If they went to supper at the Savoy his car with its chauffeur would be waiting at Mrs. Robinson's door and when they arrived at the Savoy Hotel—which was their favourite eating place—as the car entered the little courtyard the faces of the porters, the assistant managers, the managers and the head waiter would light up in smiles of pure rapture. There was no question of seeking a table. Here in a corner, secluded and delightful, was the table reserved for His Highness. A menu had been arranged in advance. The chef excelled himself. The service was impeccable and at the end it was Major Maboob who signed the bill, adding a tip that by English standards was overgenerous. This kind of life suited Mrs. Robinson down to the ground. But affairs such as this have a momentum of their own and Hari Singh thought that his association with Mrs. Robinson might be becoming too noticeable, too noticeable, that is, to the India Office, which kept a watchful eye on the doings of great Indian princes in Britain. The India Office was not swayed by any code of morality, but it was acutely conscious that Indian princes abroad should behave 'suitably'. Hari Singh sensed that the India Office was beginning to take an interest, and possibly a disapproving interest, in his affair with Mrs. Robinson. He had received no letter or communication on the matter from the India Office but one small incident had suggested to him that the powers-that-be in Whitehall were not unaware of what was going on.

The incident occurred while the Prince and Mrs. Robinson where lunching at Claridges Hotel, quietly together, attended only by the faithful Major Maboob. Sitting at the next table was a British official whom Hari Singh instantly recognised as a Permanent Secretary in the India Office. Hari Singh rose to greet his acquaintance, who reciprocated with just that touch of affability tempered with deference which one might expect. However, Hari Singh was an extremely perceptive young man and when the eye of the Permanent Secretary lighted upon Mrs. Robinson Hari Singh thought that he saw a British frost in the eyes of the Permanent Secretary, and moreover it was some minutes before the frost thawed. Hari Singh knew quite well that as a result of this unfortunate meeting the activities of the heir-presumptive of Kashmir would be made the subject of discreet debate in the India Office. It was not, as I have explained, that the India Office regarded itself in any sense as custodian of the morals of Indian princes. The India Office assumed that on their journeys to Europe the princes would go to bed with a succession of European ladies. As this was not permitted in India, it was natural that they should seek a change of diet when they travelled abroad. But the India Office were interested in the throne of Kashmir. The ruling maharajah, eccentric even by Indian royal standards, was getting old, and the India Office did not want to have Mrs. Robinson as the acknowledged or unacknowledged Queen of Kashmir.

So Hari Singh wisely departed to Paris, where he thought it would take the British Embassy some time to catch up with him, especially as he was travelling under a name other than his own. The French, of course, were delighted to have a fabulously rich Indian potentate in their midst and were only too ready to exercise their traditional talent for entertaining gentlemen visiting France.

In his concern for British officialdom Hari Singh had forgotten that he might have other parties to contend with, the shadowy people who had organised his first meeting with Mrs. Robinson. So, blissfully unaware that any plot was being hatched, Hari Singh and Mrs. Robinson took a suite at the St. James and Albany Hotel where they shared a large bedroom and a large bed. On Christmas Day they had enjoyed themselves immensely in Paris, seeing the sights and ending up in the fashionable nightclub of the year. They had retired about two in the morning and Hari Singh was stunned when, just after six o'clock, Mr. Montgau Noel Newton burst into his bedroom and shouted at the top of his voice: 'I've got you! I've got you!'

At first the prince was furious. He was accustomed to being woken by a manservant on the staff of the hotel discreetly murmuring, 'Altesse, it is nearly ten o'clock.' This man would then draw the blinds noiselessly and with the help of two accolytes bring in the prince's breakfast which consisted of coffee, croissants, ripe pears and half a bottle of dry champagne. This morning was different.

The prince's A.D.C., the adaptable Captain Arthur, lost no time in telling the prince that he had no doubt that Newton was acting on behalf of Mr. Robinson, the outraged husband of Mrs. Robinson. Mr. Robinson would undoubtedly bring a divorce action which would attract enormous publicity and probably result in the India Office declaring that, because of the scandal, Prince Hari Singh should not succeed his uncle as the ruler of Kashmir.

Prince Hari Singh then acted most unwisely. Terrified, it seems, by the threat of instant and sensational divorce proceedings, he signed two cheques on the treasury of Kashmir—we are moving, you realise, in the highest circles— explaining that one could be cashed immediately but the other would require a few days for funds to be allocated to meet it. It may be worth noting that these cheques in present-day values would amount to well over half a million pounds.

The cheque that could be cashed immediately was cashed by a Mr. William Cooper Hobbs on behalf of Messrs. Appleton, a firm of solicitors acting for Mr. Robinson. Mr. Hobbs had a strange history. He was, in fact, the firm of Appleton and Company, although he was not a solicitor, but a managing clerk. He specialised in the seamier side of the law, especially in cases involving scandal. Hobbs promptly offered Robinson twenty-five thousand pounds in cash, less Hobbs' fee of four thousand pounds, which Robinson gratefully accepted and, in a spirit of unwarranted generosity, handed to Mrs. Robinson.

It did not take Mr. Robinson long to find out that there had been two cheques, each for one hundred and fifty thousand pounds. The second cheque had been stopped by solicitors whom the prince had at last consulted, but still there was one hundred and twenty-nine thousand pounds missing on the first cheque.

Robinson then took fresh legal advice and decided to sue the Midland Bank for money received by them on his behalf. This led to the sensational civil case before Lord Darling, which we will now examine, but before we do so we should mention that Mrs. Robinson pursued Prince Hari Singh to the South of France, the prince having escaped from Paris to Monaco. With Mrs. Robinson, of course, was her faithful woman friend, who wanted to be reunited with Major Maboob. The general idea of the ladies was that the prince, Mrs. Robinson, her woman friend and Major Maboob should then take a slow but luxurious boat for India and eventually reach the prince's kingdom. There were unhappy reports that the life of the eccentric old maharajah was drawing to a close and it looked as if the party might turn up in time for Prince Hari Singh's coronation, with all the magnificent festivities that would accompany that event.

However, the shadowy crooks who engineered this entire business did not want Mrs. Robinson to go off with the prince, for they were still hoping that the prince, under pressure, would honour his second cheque. So they hired a man who was an ex-detective to pose as a British police officer who turned up in France and persuaded the French police to send a message to Mrs. Robinson that she and her friend must return to England immediately, which they did, reluctantly leaving Hari Singh in peace, poorer, it is true, by one hundred and fifty thousand pounds, but still in peace.

The case came up for hearing on the 19th November 1924 before Lord Darling and a special jury. The counsel engaged were numerous and distinguished, including that great figure Sir John Simon, who led the team of lawyers representing the Midland Bank. Lord Halsbury, K.C., led for the plaintiff, Mr. Robinson.

It was a long, fascinating but involved case, taking just over a week. The extremely complicated issues of law and of fact were not made any clearer, in my opinion, by the judge, either in his conduct of the trial or in his summing-up. Lord Darling had retired two years previously and had only returned to assist the courts in clearing a backlog of civil cases that threatened to slow down the whole process of justice in the High Court. He was renowned as a wit and his reputation in this respect was fully justified. Unfortunately, the law is not a funny business and his humorous interjections, though they tended to amuse the public gallery, also distracted the jurors from their real job of solving and deciding a most difficult matter. The profession of wit has always been most acceptable to the public and still is. At this moment their is a television and radio personality who makes a great success in his capacity as a wit and as a cook. In his case the vocation of wit blends superbly with his other gifts, but in the case of Lord Darling his wit, which bubbled and burst at the most unexpected moments, really was an unpardonable distraction.

I cannot, in the confines of this chapter, describe every

clandestine convolution that took place in the drama of Hari Singh, but at least I can mention one point that gives the atmosphere of unreality and charade that permeated the whole picture. At one point in the trial it was suggested that there was not one Mr. Robinson but two Mr. Robinsons, while at another point it was suggested that Mrs. Robinson was not Mrs. Robinson, because she was not married to Mr. Robinson – to either Mr. Robinson. This kind of elaborate hocus-pocus went on all the time.

However, after the judge had summed up on the eighth day with marked lack of clarity and lack of impartiality, he did contrive to put five questions to the jury.

These questions were: 'Were the words "pay to the order of Mr. C. Robinson, Appleton & Company £150,000" written by some person as agent for Appleton & Company?' The jury's answer to this was: 'No.'

The second question was: 'Had Appleton & Company or Hobbs any intention of transferring the entire proceeds of one hundred and fifty thousand pounds to the plaintiff?' The answer was: 'No.'

The third question was: 'Were those rights in fact ever transferred by Appleton & Company or Hobbs to the plaintiff?' The jury said, and I do not blame them, that they did not know the answer to this one.

The fourth question was, in effect, did the bank pay out the one hundred and fifty thousand pounds in accordance with the mandate they had received. The answer was: 'Yes.'

The last question was: 'Did Hobbs when he drew the money out, act under the same authority under which he paid it in?' The answer to this one was: 'Yes.'

Lord Darling was not in a co-operative mood that day and he refused practically every request made to him. Counsel suggested that as the unanswered question was, in fact, the key question, the jury should be asked to retire to see if they could come to some conclusion about it. 'No,' said the judge 'It's getting very late.' Then counsel suggested that they would be willing to accept a majority verdict. 'No,' said the judge. Finally the jury, thinking that they had given an exceptionally long spell of jury service in a complicated case, asked to be excused from further jury service. 'No,' said the judge. 'It takes much longer than this case for you to deserve that exemption, and, in any case, it's been an interesting case for you.'

We must admit that Lord Darling brightened the proceedings to the very end. For instance, when Sir John Simon said: 'I don't know how much longer the jury will be, but it is getting difficult for me to be here much later,' Lord Darling promptly replied, 'I don't expect to be here long, you had better arrange some day (for hearing points of law) within the lifetime that I may expect.'

Counsel now had to press the judge to tell them what, in fact, the jury had decided. Was it a verdict for the plaintiff or for the defendant? Lord Darling, after listening to quite a lot of legal argument, finally came down in favour of the defendants, the Midland Bank. Then, of course, there was an argument about costs most of which were awarded to the defendant with certain exceptions in favour of the plaintiff.

So ended the famous case of Hari Singh. You will be glad to hear that he survived his tribulations to become the ruler of his country. Most of the crooks were prosecuted and received prison sentences. It had been an impudent and vile blackmail and had succeeded in extorting a huge sum of money by intimidation. No divorce proceedings were, in fact, ever instituted by Mr. Robinson against the Prince.

It is said that Prince Hari Singh, though he visited Europe on many subsequence occasions, fought shy of coming to London, preferring to spend his vacations away from the cares of office in Paris, in Rome or in Cairo.

I do not think we can blame him for the fact that his choice of holiday resorts did not include the United Kingdom. His good relations with the India Office were, however, fully restored, and after his experience his Minister of Finance found it extremely difficult to get the prince to sign any cheque whatever on the treasury of his state without long and searching investigation.

6

Sky-jack

THE year 1970 was a year of startling political development throughout the world. Up to now the main ideological clash had been between the free-enterprise or capitalistic nations led by the United States and the communist countries with the twin-headed leadership of the Soviet Union and China. There were, of course, variations on this theme. Britain, for instance, had for many years pursued, either under a Conservative Government or a Labour Government, the policies of what may be termed conservative and compromise socialism which were first accepted under the Labour Government of 1945, and were given the mantle of Tory approval at the time that Lord Butler was doing the thinking and planning of the Conservative Party.

This set-up was comparatively simple. The two sides viewed each other with suspicion and distrust which were occasionally thawed by friendly approaches, mainly cultural, if it suited the book of the party concerned. Both sides engaged in active espionage to try to probe the military secrets of the other side, especially in the field of nuclear development. A new dimension was added to this activity when it was found possible to have 'spy satellites' encircling the globe and sending back photographs of the territory over which they passed.

From time to time an opportunity occurred for either side to engineer a *coup d'état* in a country aligned to the other side and there were perhaps ten such engineered coups in the 'sixties. Several countries were split in two by the determination of both parties not to yield an inch, notably Germany, Korea and Vietnam. It was an unhealthy international climate, but at least the balance of terror seemed to assure the avoidance of a third world war. When it came to the crunch, as it did for instance in Cuba, the side who were farthest from their base communications would give in at the last moment. This led to the doctrine of brinkmanship which was so favoured by Mr. Dulles, a dedicated and sincere but lamentable Secretary of the State Department in Washington. No one had the vision or authority to start building a real peace, to stop the provocative espionage, to unite the divided countries and to halt the constant attempts at subversion aided and abetted by the secret services of the two sides. The nuclear weapons which America and the Soviet Union had ready to deploy, including rockets with multiple warheads, represented a massive 'over-kill', that is to say both these powers had the immediate ability to destroy humanity as we know it. In addition to this Britain and France had an impressive nuclear capability which could not be entirely left out of international calculations.

The result of all this was that the 'sixties was a decade of uneasy peace. It was a fantastic commentary on the failure of civilisation and the failure of the Christian, Buddhist and Moslem religions that all they could achieve for the world was an incredibly expensive armed neutrality. At a time when money was urgently needed for modernising housing, for improving communications and for ensuring food for everyone, vast sums were spent on pushing forward the nuclear race. Like all evil situations it fed on itself becoming ever more bloated and obscene. The spies would return to Moscow or to Washington, to London or to Paris, with reports that some new mechanism of destruction had been invented which, of course, needed new weapons of defence and new means of attack. If there is a Satanic influence which seeks to pervert and degrade man then certainly that influence was most successful between 1960 and 1970. All the decent and natural instincts of ordinary people for freedom, for a home, for peace, for work, for leisure and for security for themselves and their children were overshadowed by the terrible facts of the unspoken war. We were all confined in a strait-jacket of fear which we ourselves had created.

This is a sombre picture of events, but I do not think it is exaggerated or inaccurate. It had, as I said, a certain stark and terrifying simplicity. Then, towards the end of the 'sixties and notably during 1970, the scene changed. All over the world it seemed new forces erupted. These forces had diverse aims. Some of them wanted simply to spread communism. They were an extension of the previous period, using different methods of direct action. However, much of the new revolution appeared to be aimed at anarchy. The message was: 'Smash the existing order entirely and whatever takes its place cannot be worse and may well be better.' The anarchists were often followers of Mao Tse-tung, who himself is a product of the unwise isolation of China by the great powers during the last fifteen years. Many of the anarchists were young, and a political programme, if one can call it that, that was so radical that it would end society as we know it appealed perhaps to their sense of adventure. Most of them had no faith to fall back on. Their minds were moved by what they believed to be frustration. In most countries it was difficult to secure congenial employment and when they did so and married and had children they feared that they were being trapped by the baits of a vast machine, that they would become data for the computers, that they would be used by the establishment for thirty years and then thrown out with a pension. This prospect did not appeal either to their idealism or to their sense of adventure. The newspapers suddenly discovered the young as a newsworthy section of society. When they rioted, or advocated complete sexual freedom, or took drugs, this was something the newspapers could write about in a sensational way that was good for sales, so we were told by implication that young men and women under thirty were a race apart and the young began to believe that this was true. The natural corollary of this was that age and experience were at a discount and a 'generation gap' was said to exist in all countries which had not noticeably been there before but was now an important reality.

To a large extent the attempt to seduce and pervert the world as it existed was uncoordinated and even unorganised, but there were men in control of world communism who saw in this new development a great new opportunity. They had to admit that if matters had been allowed to proceed along the lines of a cold war then the advent of world communism, which they sought, was going to be delayed for a long time and might never materialise. The free world had also had remarkable successes and it was by no means certain that the communist world was going to win the battle for the minds and the hearts of men. This new revolutionary insurgency presented to the directors of the communist parties a wonderful opportunity. The smashing of the establishment everywhere was the first aim of international communism, because out of chaos communism would surely come. So with cleverness and care the new torrent of revolution was channelled into directions where it could be most effectively employed and have its quickest impact on the political scene.

The first truly amazing success came in France, where the students joined in a trade-union revolt and captured the streets of Paris. Had not General de Gaulle flown to his army headquarters and secured the loyal support of the army the French nation as we know it would have ceased to exist. As it was, such was the impact of this revolution that General de Gaulle had to end his reign. The revolution of the students had toppled the most formidable figure in European politics, but it had not been able to smash the French establishment. That objective is certainly still contemplated and planned for and an attempt will be made to achieve it, probably within the next five years. In Italy the existence of a very large communist party was linked to the revolt of the young, and open rioting flares constantly in southern Italy.

Those who control the communist party machine did not wish to be linked too obviously with the student revolution, so they remained as manipulators in the background and, with great skill and perspicacity, they provided the revolutionary fervour of the 'new left' with a cover story which would at the same time conceal the manipulation and give to the rebels an immediate and practical cause. There are obvious examples of this. Throughout South America there has for many years been agitation against military dictator-

E

ships which protected the great landlords and the big commercial interests, both indigenous and foreign. The figure of Castro looms over the entire sub-continent. In certain countries the discontent and the revolutionary fervour have become acute and by introducing the technique of the sky-jack and the hi-jack the rebels were able to bring acute embarrassment to the established governments. As they were quite prepared to add murder to their list of crimes, a small number of revolutionaries could cause great havoc, but the main point was that the young revolutionaries had something immediate and practical to occupy their minds. It was all action.

In the Arab world a minor cold war existed since June 1967 which was a parallel of the world situation. Israel occupied large areas of Arab territory, including the whole of Sinai and all Jordanian territory on the west bank of the river Jordan.

Among the extreme left wing of governing circles in Syria and Iraq there was animosity towards King Hussein of Jordan, who was described as a 'stooge of the West'. This was most unfair. King Hussein had received into his country and given shelter to over a million Arab refugees, an act of unparalleled generosity which no other Arab country had even approached in its immensity. During the June War of 1967 it was the army of King Hussein who fought most bravely and tenaciously against the Israelis and succeeded in killing more Israelis than were accounted for by all the other Arab nations combined. Nevertheless, perhaps because he is a king, and perhaps because he has immense popularity among his own people and the dedicated loyalty of his army, King Hussein has many enemies. So it was decided that the British-sponsored resolution of December 1967, which called for an evacuation of the Israeli Army of occupied territory to agreed and guaranteed frontiers was no longer acceptable to the Left. They saw that peace might be achieved if this resolution ever became effective—and they did not want peace. Peace would have entrenched the establishment on both sides and their aim was the destruction of the establishment. In this situation the communists, and especially the representatives of Chinese communism, saw their opportunity. Hence the creation of a Palestine Liberation Front under such leaders as the revolutionary George Habash.

Now, the objective of this new movement, which also had a more moderate section led by Yasser Arafat, was in practical terms not obtainable, but it was very cleverly disguised. 'All we want,' they said, 'is for Palestine to be freed, so that Arab and Jew can live in peace in their homeland.' It was an idea calculated to appeal to visionaries everywhere. But, of course, hidden under the cloak of words was the fact that this entailed the destruction of the sovereign state of Israel as it at present exists. The commanders, Chinese financed and Chinese advised, knew quite well that the goal could not be achieved. This did not worry them in the least. Their aim was not success but chaos, in the certain hope that out of chaos their movement could seize power.

The Popular Front for the Liberation of Palestine set up its headquarters in Beirut—well away from the firing line—and Mr. Habash flitted round the area between Beirut, Baghdad and Damascus, occasionally making lightning visits to Jordan. Then the back-room boys of this new Near Eastern revolution thought up a grandiose plan which would really catch the world's headlines and rivet the political attention of the world on the revolutionaries and their cause. They wanted to show that the Near Eastern situation was no longer dominated or controlled by President Nasser, King Hussein and Mrs. Meir. They wanted to demonstrate that it was the Popular Front for the Liberation of Palestine that was the dynamic force in the Middle East. In order to do this they decided to sky-jack one American, one Swiss, and one British plane and to take these planes to a desert airstrip in Jordan. It is a tribute to the ruthlessness of their planning that they succeeded in doing this, capturing a Swissair DC8, a Trans-World Airline Boeing 707, and a VC10 of B.O.A.C. The planes, with over two hundred passengers, were held at Revolutionary Airfield. Immediately around the planes were the irregular troops of Mr. Habash, heavily armed, and they were very shortly surrounded in their turn by the troops of the Jordanian Army and their tanks.

Now comes the massive and terrible intimidation. Each plane was fitted with enough dynamite to explode the plane and to murder all the passengers inside. Lines were laid so that each plane could be blown up in turn by the commandos from their entrenched positions outside. The threat was one of the most terrible ever made by a small number of men holding the world to ransom. Messages were flashed by the commandos to New York, London and to Berne fixing a deadline for blowing up the planes, and incidentally, murdering the passengers as well as the crew. The blackmail was clear for all to read and to see. The commandos demanded the immediate release of all their prisoners held in Israeli and Jordanian gaols. They also demanded the release of one prisoner held by the police in London. This was an unappetising young lady named Leila Khaled, who, with an accomplice, had tried to hi-jack an Israeli plane as it flew over Britain. Miss Khaled's accomplice, who was a man, was shot dead on the plane, but Miss Khaled was merely bound and taken prisoner.

At first it seemed that there was a dangerous possibility that the Israelis and the Swiss might do a separate deal with the commandos. In order to prevent this, the British Government, who in this instance held the trump card, came to a quick agreement with the American Government that all the passengers and crew of the three airliners must be released before any of the commando prisoners would be released and the Swiss Government was persuaded to co-operate, the Israeli Government taking up a position of its own but in fact 'co-operating without compromise'.

The position now was very much stronger. The commandos never expected to be faced with a united front. But they still had some cards in their hand. The commandos knew very well that Miss Khaled in London would come to no harm. She might have to remain there for some time, but she would be well treated and there was no risk whatever of her being murdered by the British authorities or ill-treated in any way. The British, Swiss and American governments were much less certain that the commandos would not press the button that would blow up the planes and result in the mass murder of the passengers and the crews.

Eventually the commandos decided that their ultimate bluff had been called. They were not prepared to murder two hundred and eight American, British, Swiss and Israeli civilians and so almost certainly bring immediate retaliation on the spot from the governments concerned. They took the passengers and crews off the planes and marshalled them into waiting trucks as prisoners. Then a scene perhaps never before witnessed by anyone took place. Vindictive and intent on colossal destruction, the commandos pressed the button that ignited the charge to each plane in turn. For the first time the world knew beyond peradventure that the planes had actually been treated with a massive charge of dynamite. The waiting prisoners, huddled in their trucks, saw the giant aeroplanes blown up one by one, the wreckage shooting into the clear Jordanian sky, so that in a matter of minutes nothing but charred rubble remained. It was the most sinister and outrageous challenge to established authority by the forces of subversion that the world had witnessed since the last war.

After some parley the Jordanian Army let the commandos through their lines and allowed them to take the prisoners off to an unknown destination. There was still an uneasy peace between the guerrillas and the Jordanian Government. However, King Hussein realised that the blowing up of the planes was a challenge to his authority that he could not conceivably overlook. On the advice of President Nasser, with whom he had good relations, he had shown extraordinary tolerance and patience with the commandos on the assumption that their aim in the long run was the same as his aim, namely a burning desire to fight the Israeli aggressors and invaders. The blowing up of the planes showed only too clearly that this was not the real aim at all. The real aim was to sabotage the tentative peace negotiations that had the support both of President Nasser and King Hussein and to make it clear to the world that Hussein was no longer master in his own country.

The king decided to act and, as always on these occasions,

he went among his troops addressing them and explaining what had happened. The army had been eager to smash the guerrillas for many months and battle was joined throughout Jordan and notably in the capital Amman between the Jordanian Army and the well-organised and well-armed guerrilla forces.

On the following night I was interviewed by Barry Westmore on Southern Television on the situation in Jordan. Talking to people in the studio before the interview I realised that, among the young people at any rate, there was a belief that this was the end of the king. The revolutionary forces would triumph and King Hussein would be fortunate to escape to the Dorchester Hotel in London with his life. I cannot help feeling a little pleased with the fact that in answer to the first question put to me by my very able and amiable interrogator I replied, according to the transcript which I have obtained: 'Yes, I know what is going to happen. The king is going to smash the guerrilla movement in Jordan.' Barry Westmore then said: 'No doubt about that whatever?' And I replied: 'No doubt at all.' For once the political prophecy was correct.

The guerrillas put up a stout resistance but within a week the Jordanian Army had taken twenty thousand prisoners and broken the back of the guerrilla army in Amman, in the south and in Irbid and the other border towns of the north. When it appeared that the Jordanian Army was going to win, Syria attempted to stab her neighbour in the back by sending a large tank force over the border to fight King Hussein's men. The king's commander-in-chief immediately detached a tank force to deal with the threat and this tank force inflicted a humiliating defeat on the large Syrian mobile force which had to escape as best as it could back to the security of its own country, leaving over fifty tanks destroyed and burning in Jordanian hands.

So all the gloomy partial prophesies were falsified and King Hussein was again master of Jordan. Meantime President Nasser had been working continuously to prevent further divisions in the Arab world. He called a conference in Cairo to which King Hussein, who has never lacked courage, flew in person. The result was a peace agreement of unparalleled generosity to the defeated guerrillas. Their prisoners were released, their lives were spared, great numbers were disarmed and the remainder were packed off to the front line against Israel, which for so long they had been protesting was their dearest ambition.

Meanwhile the governments concerned in the matter, whose nationals were no longer sky-jacked but were still hijacked during the six-day 'civil war' in Jordan, had been faced with one dilemma after another. When fierce fighting broke out in Amman the prisoners of the commandos were in real danger. Captain Cyril Goulborn of B.O.A.C. on a sheet of lined paper torn from an exercise book managed to get this message through to the British Embassy in Jordan:

'We are being properly treated in the circumstances and have food. Conditions, however, are very crowded and some people are in constant fear. All B.O.A.C. passengers are in good spirits. But please get us out as soon as possible. Each passing day things become more difficult.'

Reading between the lines of this message was a fairly desperate plea for help. There seemed to be a real possibility of Anglo-American intervention. The British Army had a considerable force available on its base in Cyprus, while the American Sixth Fleet, reinforced with large detachments of Marines, was cruising off the coast of Lebanon and Israel. However, the news of the king's victory made any intervention, which would probably have been undesirable, also unnecessary.

The defeat of the guerrillas had been specially aimed at Habash and his Popular Front. Habash had fled to Syria when the fighting broke out, but was said, from time to time, to be back in Jordan surveying the ruins of his cause and the desperate plight of the guerrillas who had put their faith in him. Now Yasser Arafat emerged as the most commanding figure in the commando movement and the only option left to the commandos was to return all the prisoners to Israel, America, Britain and Switzerland in the hope that the political prisoners held by the European powers, other than Israel, would be returned as promised. Especially were the guerillas anxious to free Leila Khaled. In due course all the passengers and crews were flown out to the British base in Cyprus and from there sent on to their various destinations. The small number of political prisoners concerned, including Miss Khaled, were flown back either to Cairo or Beirut. The commandos were hoping that the arrival of Miss Khaled in Cairo would evoke a popular demonstration in favour of the Popular Front, but in the meantime President Nasser had died from overwork given to the causes he believed in. Hardly anyone in Cairo noticed the return of Leila Khaled. They were mourning their lost leader.

This, in outline, is the fantastic story of the greatest modern intimidation of recent years. It shows with painful clarity that established authority everywhere is faced with an entirely new technique of mischief and revolution. It is almost impossible by any known method to prevent kidnapping if it is organised by armed and ruthless men. So far it has not been possible effectively to prevent determined sky-jacking, though now methods are being devised which make it much more difficult. Certainly both the hi-jack and the sky-jack will be employed again by the forces of disruption. One can only hope that in the end they will be defeated.

At least now we should recognise the danger and know that intimidation of a new and ruthless kind is going to be rampant in our world which we have either to submit to or to defy and defeat. When there is failure in one area, as in Jordan, similar methods and a similar cloak of a cause will flare up elsewhere as they have now done in the province of Quebec, the aim there being chaos and the destruction of the establishment again skilfully disguised as a political liberation movement.

7

The Grasshopper

IT WAS the sheerest accident that accounted for my meeting Lim Chuen, who controlled the gold and narcotics racket in Singapore between the wars.

I do not know how he came to be called the Grasshopper unless it was his habit when he was listening—or not answering—of retaining complete immobility as if he was frozen alive. At such moments his handsome Mongolian features would assume a mask of absolute impassivity. Only the brown eyes were never still. They darted here and there, scrutinising, assessing, plotting. The brain too was active. One was acutely conscious that this man was thinking ahead and thinking fast.

Then, when Lim Chuen had absorbed the whole picture, he would suddenly move, springing from his chair and pacing his room, restless, fired, it seemed, by a dynamo he could not contain. It was the acute contrast between his immobility and his restlessness that struck one at a first meeting. When he was in action his expression was no longer a mask. Every sentiment was written in his face, which could show pleasure, anger, disdain or menace, with dramatic power. He was a formidable person. It was quite impossible to ignore him even for a moment. He imposed the tough pattern of his mind on all those with whom he dealt. He was accustomed to having his own way and had become a natural autocrat.

I never expected to meet him face to face. I had heard of him, of course, by reputation. It was known in the 'twenties and 'thirties that a most lucrative business in smuggling gold and narcotics (especially opium made up as morphine in bricks stamped 999) existed between Tokyo, Hong

Kong, Singapore and the West. It was said that the Grasshopper ruled this criminal empire with a rod of iron. This
would have entailed no more than an unending battle between
the police and the Grasshopper and his men if that had
been the end of the story. But it was not the end. There had
been too many 'suicides' among young airline pilots and
even hostesses to be credible. The police believed that
in every case the dead man or girl had been lured into
the service of the Grasshopper. Suspected of disloyalty,
informing, or taking an unagreed profit, they were murdered,
but in the most subtle way. The newspapers hinted that the
Grasshopper and his associates were masters of the art of
murder disguised as suicide, that they had studied this very
special technique for years and had brought it to perfection
so that the 'suicide' would completely mask the murder,
and not even the best forensic scientists could say with
certainty that, in fact, murder had been done.

I flew down from Bangkok on my business as a lawyer.
A large consignment of tinned milk had been received by my
client in a shocking condition, so that it was unsaleable, and
this entailed a loss to the purchaser of some thousands
of pounds. The American firm who had sold the consignment
professed to be completely puzzled by the whole affair. The
milk, they said, was fresh and properly tinned on despatch
from Singapore. How then came it about that on arrival
four days later it was unsaleable? Nevertheless we opened
a sample of cans and four out of five exploded in our faces,
emitting a revolting smell and a stream of dark yellow 'milk'.

My client was Chinese and he did not want the long delay
that would have been inevitable if he had brought an
action in Bangkok and attempted to serve the writ at the
vendor's offices in Singapore. He thought that a sudden,
unannounced visit to the culprits by Gerald Sparrow, the
British lawyer, could achieve a quick settlement. He was
right. It did. I took with me half a dozen cans of the con-
taminated milk and insisted on opening them on the desk
of the managing director of the reputable firm which had sold
them. It occurred to me that this was something of a gamble.
What would happen if, in fact, there were good patches in the

consignment and my samples had been culled from such a patch? I could see the triumphant smiles of our opponents. But, to my intense delight, every single can exploded and emitted its atrocious odour and its stream of dank, bad milk.

How much was involved? I was asked. I produced the consignment note. The sum was four thousand eight hundred and ninety pounds. Then my client had paid six hundred and eighty pounds duty. Then he had lost the goodwill of several good customers.

'How much will you settle for?'

'Seven thousand pounds.'

'We will pay up to five thousand pounds.'

'I will accept six thousand five hundred pounds, no less.'

The managing director, a large blond man with sideburns, in his middle fifties, unlocked the drawer of his desk, took out a cheque book and wrote a cheque for the sum I was willing to take as a compromise.

'Thank you. Here is a discharge.'

'Good. How about lunch? At my club. You can tell me what the news is in Bangkok.'

My Chinese client had been fairly astute in the method he employed to get his money back. After paying my fee and expenses he still had over six thousand pounds. He was well satisfied and when Christmas came the next month he sent me two turkeys, six bottles of Beehive brandy, a box of Manilla cigars and ten yards of Thai silk (for a dress for Madame). Thus was business conducted at this time very far east of Suez.

My first night in Singapore I turned over some notes I had made before leaving, in my bedroom in the Raffles Hotel, Room 24. I saw that my Chinese client had said: 'Suggest you meet Mr. Lim Chuen, influential business man. His house 221 Richmond Road.' I had no idea what was the purpose of this note, but, as I had nothing better to do and did not want to explore the cabarets of the town, I looked up Mr. Lim Chuen in the telephone book. There he was. *Lim Chuen, Exporter,* Prince of Wales Mansion, first floor. Obviously his office, and here was his house—The Retreat, 221 Richmond Road. The telephone number (not ex-directory, I noticed with mild surprise) 5557. I rang 5557. A girl answered.

'Mr. Lim Chuen not at home. Back at eight. Your name, please?'

I gave my name. The voice apparently thought a moment.

'Where you stay?'

'Raffles Hotel.'

'Mr. Lim Chuen ring you there eight o'clock. O.K.?'

'O.K. Thank you.'

'Don't mention it.'

I did not mention it to anyone because as I was making the call I remembered that this was the Lim Chuen, who was said to be the richest and most powerful gangster in South-East Asia. Why my client wanted me to meet him I could not imagine. But I thought that a visit to Lim Chuen at home might be interesting and it promised to make the evening pass very quickly.

At eight precisely the telephone rang. I was in the restaurant. The boy brought me the telephone to my table.

'Is that Mr. Sparrow, the English lawyer from Bangkok?'

'Yes, Mr. Lim Chuen?'

'I am Mr. Lim Chuen. I like to meet you. . . .'

'Right. Tomorrow.?'

'Now is always the best time. I send my car for you. Ten minutes arrive.'

'Please make it half an hour, as I am having my dinner.'

'Of course, eight-thirty. My man wait for you.'

I did not know quite why I felt a sense of excitement at the prospect of meeting Lim Chuen. Both the girl and Lim Chuen, though their English was indifferent, seemed to me to be very much on the spot. They were quick and decisive and I was prepared to believe that Lim Chuen let no grass grow under his feet. Whether he was the monster the newspapers hinted at it was impossible to tell—yet.

As I finished my meal—a cold consommé, a sole, half a bottle of chablis and some strawberries flown in from north Burma, with coffee served by a black boy in Turkish uniform—my waiter came up again.

'Car wait for you, Tuan.'

I finished my coffee and strolled to the revolving gates of

the hotel and down the steps that were lined with frangipani. The flower gives an overwhelming scent at night. I felt content and at peace. I had had a good day and now perhaps I should have a diverting evening. .

The chauffeur was Chinese, of course. I did not expect to find any Malays or Indians in the Lim Chuen ménage. Nor did I. Like his master, the driver was polite and efficient. He sprang out to open the door intent to reach the handle before I did. He drove fast but carefully. We swung off the main road into a drive, travelled a couple of hundred yards and there was the house, large, lighted. In front of the door sat a watchman, a stout Chinese. He had two dogs on a leash. It occurred to me that it would not have been easy for an unwelcome guest to gain admittance to number 221.

The girl came to the door. I recognised her voice at once. She was quite lovely. She was wearing a European evening dress, a cocktail dress I suppose, in black embroidered with beads. She was slim, tall for a Chinese, very fair with eyes that set off the curve of her high cheek-bones. Her lips were full and I thought sensuous, but her manner was quiet, friendly, with no hint of flirtation. She smiled.

'Welcome. My uncle is waiting for you.'

'Uncle?' I thought this was probably a sop to my British prejudices. This young woman was a mistress. She had the assurance of a girl desired by a man of power. I followed her into the study.

Lim Chuen rose to greet me, his handsome face wreathed in smiles.

'Delighted to meet you. We hear so much about you from our friends.'

He might have been an ambassador putting a visitor at his ease. I realised that, gangster or not, murderer or innocent, Lim Chuen had risen to the top by force of an impelling personality and—yes, I had to admit it—great charm.

Lim Chuen talked of mutual friends in Singapore, Hong Kong and Bangkok. I noticed that he moved easily, in conversation at any rate, between the great Eastern cities. I had the distinct impression that he regarded the Lion City of

Singapore, the Abode of the Angels which is Bangkok, and the flowered island of Hong Kong as all part of his grand design. He was not an insular Chinese.

After about an hour a servant brought in champagne and smoked-salmon sandwiches, both expensive and difficult to come by in Singapore. The conversation became more lively. The young woman joined us and I noticed that she no longer kept up the uncle pretence. That was just for show until they had seen me. When they discovered that I, too, was human they dropped the subterfuge. Lim Chuen gave me a very fine Havana cigar and the young woman sat in a corner smoking French cigarettes. 'A present from Saigon,' she said.

I made a move as if to rise and be on my way, but Lim Chuen laid a restraining hand on my knee. 'Just a minute. I have a suggestion to make to you. . . .'

'Yes.'

'The police are enquiring into a shipment of spare motor parts that arrived in this country a week ago. They were consigned to my firm to be shipped to Surabaya. Apparently some narcotics have been found cleverly concealed in the spare parts. Morphine. Mr. Sparrow, I know nothing of this business at all. I want you to protect my interest. Stay a few days until the matter is settled. See that I am not involved. I have here a contribution towards your fee.'

Lim Chuen produced a wad of fifty-dollar bills from his hip pocket.

'Please see the police commissioner on my behalf and tell him I know nothing of this matter.'

It was a dilemma. Should I act for him? The newspapers had branded him as a master smuggler and hinted at murder. But was he to be tried by the newspapers? Was he not, like every accused person, entitled to the protection of counsel? The great Erskine had laid it down that 'on no account must a lawyer interpose his own, perhaps mistaken, opinion of the guilt of his client to his client's detriment'. I accepted.

I extended my stay to a week. I saw the deputy commissioner of police, who said, 'We are sure it is his but we have no evidence and don't look like getting any. The informers have gone cold on us.'

I told Lim Chuen the gist of what had occurred at the meeting. He seemed relieved. He paid me the balance of the fee. We said goodbye. He came to see me off at the airport and his engaging girl came too, waving her small lace handkerchief as she stood there on the runway.

I never expected to see Lim Chuen again. But a month later he turned up, unannounced, at my office in Suriwongse Road, Bangkok. My clerk, Nai Udorm, showed him in. His manner was still suave and assured, but I noticed at once that he looked worried in a way he had never shown during the little incident of the morphine in the spare motor parts.

I asked him to sit down and the boy brought us in iced coffee.

'Mr. Sparrow. I have great trouble. A young steward on Imperial Airways has hanged himself in a Chinese hotel in Singapore. Gold bars were found stitched into his waistcoat. The police have, as yet, taken no steps, but the newspapers, especially the vernacular press, have been most unpleasant, saying that I and my men hanged the man and faked the suicide. But the doctor certified suicide. It is completely absurd.'

Mr. Lim Chuen certainly was in trouble. He seemed to attract the most remarkable coincidences. Was it just possible that, rich and successful, he was being made the victim of a vendetta by people who disliked him or even hated and feared him?

I looked at his face more carefully than I had done before. If there was cruelty and murder there it was most dexterously concealed. I saw nothing but a bland, able Chinese tycoon, worried and even outraged. Was it all an act?

Mr. Lim Chuen wanted me to go and 'have a talk with the commissioner' again.

I refused. 'It would be a great mistake. They may have no evidence at all. If you are completely innocent, as you say, the fact that I had flown in from Bangkok would suggest that you are much more nervous than you should be.'

Mr. Lim Chuen thought over this. 'You may be right.'

'I am right. If you find that they are going to charge you, and if I have your written assurance on oath before your ancestors that you are innocent, I will come and defend you. Until then, wait.'

Mr. Lim Chuen took a piece of notepaper from my desk and wrote: 'I, Lim Chuen, do swear on the cherished memory of my ancestors that I have never murdered anyone, or caused anyone to be murdered.' And he signed it.

It was over a month before the summons came. I flew to Singapore. Mr. Lim Chuen had been arrested. The charge—murder.

The day after my arrival I met him at the police station. He was still dignified, quiet, authoritative. I went through the evidence with him. It proved that Lim Chuen had had an interest in the gold found on the dead man's body. But did it prove murder? I thought not. The doctor who had certified suicide stuck to his decision. Mr. Lim Chuen, of course, had been nowhere near the scene of the crime. I felt the police were waiting for Lim Chuen to hang himself by some act of panic. That was what I had to prevent.

At the post mortem the evidence seemed clear that the young man had strangled himself by hanging. The police doctor said that death was consistent with this theory. No one explained the gold that had been found on the body. But the gold was a strong point in Lim Chuen's favour. The Grasshopper's men, if they had been the murderers, would scarcely have left so valuable a prize on the corpse. Besides, at this point there was no evidence other than that of strangulation by self-inflicted hanging.

The strange events that followed were due entirely to the perseverance or obstinacy of a police doctor. He insisted on examining the stomach of the dead man and of searching the corpse once more. What he found between the large left toenail and the skin was the mark of a needle insertion. That was what he had been looking for. He then applied the latest tests to the stomach contents and was able to prove an overdose of morphine. So the young man had been put to sleep first, then hanged. This was very much in the suspected pattern of the Lim Chuen killings. The net was closing. But still why the gold bars? Then the bars themselves were examined. They were clever fakes. So had the murdered man been cheating his employers with fake gold, having stolen the genuine bars himself and sold them? It seemed that this was the real explanation.

The police thought they had enough to pay a first visit to 221 Richmond Road. They wanted to question Lim Chuen. They had a very long file on his activities and they were quite sure he could not survive a long and gruelling examination.

But Mr. Lim Chiuen was not at home. Where had he gone? The young woman said she had no idea. Perhaps the police could tell her?

The police dug for information. All their informers were told that there was a reward of five thousand dollars for information that would lead to the arrest of Lim Chuen. This time the underworld of the informers erupted. Every informer seemed to have different information. Mr. Lim Chuen was in Switzerland (where he had a bank account) on business. Mr. Lim Chuen was in San Francisco. Mr. Lim Chuen was in Australia. But, in fact, Mr. Lim Chuen had gone underground in Singapore, not a hundred yards from the Central Police Station. There, in hiding, he made certain dispositions of his property—in cash. He gave the young woman, whose name I discovered was Chieng, a million Straits dollars. He left one old discarded wife—the woman who had come with him from China when all the world was young—two hundred thousand dollars. He left a quarter of a million for the preservation of the family burial place and the schooling of three young sons.

And he wrote me a letter. It had, I think, a certain classical quality.

'Dear Mr. Sparrow.

'The police are becoming most oppressive and I do not like being questioned by people of that kind. I have made certain dispositions which I ask you to see are carried out. You will find them in an attachment to this letter. I also ask you to

F

accept the enclosed fee, for I realise that it was not easy for you to represent me and I am grateful to you for doing so.

'Life has lost its savour for me. I have no intention of being imprisoned or disgraced and so I am ringing down the curtain. I join my ancestors, Sir, a little prematurely but without regrets.

'I send you again my gratitude and cordial respects.

'Yours very truly,
Lim Chuen'

He was found dead at number 221 Richmond Road. He had returned there from his hiding place and put himself to sleep in the great bed which was his pride.

The case aroused immense interest. The press of Malaya ran all kinds of stories. Lim Chuen was depicted as a monster who had executed not once but many times.

The police had now smashed the gang and arrested some of the minor figures in the drama, but not the girl, Chieng. Apparently she knew nothing of his business activities. 'I was strictly his love-woman,' she told the police, and the police had to admit this was true. She was allowed to remain at number 221, which a year later she sold for a very high price. With its three garages, four bathrooms, billiard room and swimming pool it was indeed desirable. A business rival of Lim Chuen, in the best Chinese tradition, bought it. But he did not buy the girl as well. She was not a fixture, it seemed.

Of course, I had to go and carry out my duty of winding up his affairs and seeing that the Grasshopper's considerable fortune was distributed as he had directed. This entailed meeting Chieng who was dressed in—very expensive—black that suited her immensely and did not quite subdue her warm and instant appeal.

I showed her the list of bequests and she smiled. 'Yes, I know, but that is only a half of it.'

'What do you mean?'

'Every amount is duplicated by a similar amount in my name in three Chinese banks. It was his money. I merely held it for him. He did not want to pay unnecessary tax.'

'So the actual estate was nearly three million?'

'A little more . . .'

'Well, if there is anything I can do to help you, please let me know.'

She looked at me with a disconcerting frankness, but said nothing. Then, almost as an aside, she said: 'I like you to advise me on investment. We can correspond by letter. Will you do that?'

I said yes, I would do that.

The most sensational of the Malay dailies ran a story, that a rival of Lim Chuen had planted the guilty evidence on his rival. This was the man who had bought number 221 Richmond Road. It was conceivable, but I thought most unlikely. I do not think that Lim Chuen would have submitted to being framed. He was too proud and too determined a character for that.

I parted from Chieng, dining with her on my last evening. She said goodbye gravely and I did not expect to see her again, though I knew she might write about the investment of her money. But just as Lim Chuen had turned up in Bangkok, so now did his 'love-woman'.

She came into my office like some orchidaceous creature, drifting an expensive perfume which I noticed she always favoured.

She was a widow no longer. Smiling and radiant now, she talked of the future.

'I want to travel, but first you must show me Siam. All its wonders, the north as well. The sapphire and ruby mines, the teak forests, the elephants, the palaces, the temples. Will you do that?'

Again I said I would do that. I realised that Chieng was feeling her way towards an affair, perhaps towards marriage, but that I did not want. I did not understand the Chinese people as I understood the Siamese. They were to me too much of a mystery. But I showed her all she wanted to see and she would clutch her minute hands in ecstasy if shown something really lovely, the sunrise in Chiengmai or the Temple of the Dawn shimmering in the light of early morning in Bangkok before the heat came. A white ghost of a temple across the brown waters of the Menam Chow Phya river that brings life to the whole country.

When it was all over she said: 'So let's be friends—always.'

'I should like that. Did Lim Chuen kill those who opposed him?'

'Of course. That is why he took his own life rather than risk disgrace.'

'I am glad you told me.'

Again I never thought I should see her again, but each year she visited me. She did not marry but had some lovers, mainly English.

Murder implacable, relentless, deliberate and most cunningly executed can seldom have had so strange a sequence.

I have always been pleased that I undertook the Grasshopper's defence. It has sometimes occurred to me since that if he had not, in his own words, rung down the curtain, I might have got him off. But whether the sword of justice would then have fallen from its scabbard I do not know.

8

Two Blackmailers

THE word blackmail first seems to have been used to describe tribute exacted by freebooters for protection and immunity. In its modern connotation it usually means forcing a victim to pay money by the threat of revealing discreditable secrets if he does not pay up.

In this chapter I am going to present to you two cases of blackmail, the first arising out of an ingenious fraud against the bank that employed him by a young Scottish clerk, and the second involving one of those rare men of a very bright plumage with social background and charm and 'presence' who contrive, by blackmail and other devices, to lead the life of a millionaire for many years until at last they become too arrogant and careless and the law brings them down.

In the first case Thomas Peterson Goudie, who was twenty-nine, and employed as a clerk in the Bank of Liverpool, managed, by great ingenuity, to embezzle a sum of over one hundred and sixty thousand pounds from his employers. In my first book in this series, *The Great Swindlers,* published thirteen years ago, I described in detail the methods by which Goudie succeeded in passing a large number of cheques, which he had forged, through the account of Mr. Hudson, a very rich man, who had founded the famous soap firm. Now I want to deal with a different aspect of this case. I would like to describe the way in which Goudie became the victim of a gang of blackmailers.

Goudie was a lank, lean and somewhat raw young Scot, but he was extremely clever. He also discovered, almost by accident, that he was a natural-born forger. He could reproduce any signature at sight and the reproductions that he made were faultless. He had known for some years that he possessed this rare and peculiar gift, but it never occurred to him to make use of it. Honesty was part of the fabric of life in the family he came from, just as religion was. When Goudie moved from Glasgow to Liverpool it was the great adventure, the first step up the English ladder. This was the turn of the century—1901, to be exact—and we must remember that the great provincial cities at this time, especially perhaps Liverpool, as the greatest port after London, promised all kinds of opportunities to a dedicated and clever young man. It was not impossible that after some years of apprenticeship he might travel as a cashier or even as an assistant manager to Cairo, to Hong Kong, to Singapore, or to Cape Town. The empire presented a vast field of opportunity for the enterprising.

Goudie's character, which, on the face of it, was impeccable (he brought with him excellent references from Scotland), had one small but, as it turned out, fatal flaw. He loved to bet on racehorses. He had done so since he was a boy of fifteen in very small amounts and he gradually came to know a good deal about the racing scene in Britain. He could identify the great stables such as those owned by the king, by Lord Lonsdale, by Lord Rosebery and the Duke of Devonshire. He knew something about the fashionable trainers and he knew the capabilities of the leading jockeys. In addition to this, Goudie carefully stored in his mind a lot of racing lore. Although up to now he had always had to place his small bets without visiting a race-course, through his reading he knew most of the major race-courses intimately, including the 'Park' courses that surround London. He collected information on records and was quite shrewd in assessing the importance of the going, the effect of the weight carried by each horse, and the distance over which it was likely to win. It was extremely unusual for a young bank clerk, starting his career, to have such an intense outside hobby and, of course, racing and betting was a very dangerous hobby for a bank clerk to indulge in.

I think I should say here that my own interest in racing

has taught me that there are two kinds of gamblers. There are people, like myself, who are shocked when they lose even quite small sums and immediately stop betting. We are not really gamblers at all. We like to be given an interest in a race. We don't expect to win. We regard the money betted as lost and if we do win we are quietly gratified and surprised.

The genuine gambler is an entirely different kind of man. He will gamble on anything. For him it is an addiction. At least a portion of genuine gamblers have a masochistic streak and derive some strange pleasure from losing money. Perhaps unconsciously they are cocking a snook at the money emblem which tends to dominate all our lives to the exclusion of better things. However this may be, the real gambler never stops. If there are six races on the card and he has lost on five races he will plunge with all the money he has with him on the last race and it must be admitted that this kind of courage is often rewarded. When it is he enjoys a thrill and a satisfaction which your careful, cautious punter can never know. It is no good saying to a gambler: 'You are going to ruin yourself.' He probably knows that already. He knows that he will have long periods of poverty, brightened by short spells of carefree affluence. He likes it that way. The payment of the rates, the electric-light bill, the butcher and the grocer does not worry him at all. It follows from this that when he is married he is a somewhat trying husband. But Goudie was not married, he had no one to ruin but himself.

I used the word addiction to describe the spell which gambling has over the real devotee. It is not too strong a term. If you say to a heroin addict: 'You will be dead within two years,' he will reply: 'I would rather be dead within two years with heroin than live fifteen years without it.' There is no meeting of the minds between the free men and the addict.

Goudie had charge of the bank accounts from A to H and he picked Mr. Hudson's account for his forgeries with an unerring eye. Mr. Hudson, it seemed, relied absolutely on the bank for the correctness of his bi-annual statements, and, believe it or not, Mr. Hudson did not know to within one or two thousand pounds how much in credit his account was on any given day.

Goudie started his embezzlement in the smallest possible way. Through losing small bets he had got into debt to the extent of fifty pounds and was afraid that his bookmaker would tell his manager. So he forged a cheque for one hundred pounds, paid off his debts and betted with the balance, putting the whole of the fifty pounds that remained on a horse which he believed had been kept back for a certain race at Newmarket. Goudie's information was that this was going to be a big betting coup by the stable concerned, which was known to be a betting stable governed by a betting trainer. The horse started at sixteen to one, and it romped home. Goudie had won eight hundred pounds plus his original stake money.

So this was it. This was the easy and clever way to affluence. He had no difficulty in injecting the one hundred pounds back into Mr. Hudson's account and for a week or so he intended to tempt providence no further—but he was a betting man. Before very long he was embezzling in hundreds and whenever he could get away at the week-end he would take the train to Newmarket, or Sandown, or Ascot or Epsom. He betted in cash with five pounds in gold sovereigns, occasionally stepping up the amount to ten, twenty or fifty pounds. Always it was cash and there was an unending flow of the money.

There has always been an evil, criminal fringe in the racing business because the nature of the sport makes this inevitable. So much money is involved and can be easily obtained if one has the right information—and if nothing goes wrong. But these are big ifs. Really accurate information is extremely difficult to come by. Stables who are on to a good thing usually guard their secret like apprehensive clams, and something may very easily go wrong. The best horse may fail to start. The jockey may be hemmed in at the turn before entering the straight and be unable to break through, or he may have to take too long a way round the field as there is no opening on the rails. All horses tend to be unpredictable and highly bred racehorses are often extremely temperamental. When horses grow older they have their days. On their day they like to race. If it is not their day nothing will persuade them to give of their best. Male horses are often upset by female horses in the paddock and female horses are subject to hazards which we need not go into. Then the distant punter has to take the English climate into account. The forecast may be dry and sunny, but, as we know, forecasts are not always correct and heavy going may ruin the chance of one horse and enormously enhance the chance of another. I once owned a racing pony that could only run decently in a monsoon. With two inches of water on the ground it could swim faster than any horse alive, but on normal going it was, to put it kindly, a very ordinary animal.

All these considerations, of course, were taken into account by Goudie, but they did not in the least deter him. He plunged on and became well known to the cash book-makers on the courses he patronised. So the inevitable happened.

Three of the most unpleasant characters that one could imagine began to notice the affluent young Mr. Goudie, who seemed to have a never-ending flow of money. They were Burge, an ex-prize-fighter who was the bully boy of the gang, a man called Mances who lived at the Charing Cross Hotel, and Laurence Abraham Marks who was a disreputable little back-street bookmaker carrying on business at Adelphi Terrace, Liverpool.

One day—it was a Friday—Goudie returned to his lodgings and there, sitting together, were Marks, Mances and Burge. They had presented a card and the landlady had allowed them to come in out of the rain.

When Goudie entered they said not a word, just staring at him, waiting for him to make the first move.

In the end he did so, saying: 'Who are you and what do you want?'

It was Mr. Marks who replied: 'We know all about you. You are a clerk employed at the Bank of Liverpool. You have been embezzling for months. You are a gambler and you are losing heavily. Now, Mr. Goudie, this is not sensible. We have the information. You place your bets through us and you will have much better results.'

Goudie thought for a moment and said: 'And if I don't?' Marks smiled, and Burge, the ex-prize-fighter, fidgeted in his seat as if he wanted to do something but was not allowed to do it. Marks replied very smoothly: 'Do not let us go into that, Mr. Goudie. You know and we know what will happen. Let's be friends.'

It was blackmail, a terrifying intimidation. Goudie knew that if he put one foot out of step at any time Burge would beat him up and that might be a very unpleasant experience. Only as a last resort would the gang inform the bank manager, because that would probably lead to Goudie's dismissal and dry up the river of never-ending gold, but Goudie did not doubt that if he defied them the gang, in anger and frustration, would bring about his downfall.

So Goudie had to carry on with his forgeries and increase them to incredible amounts. Cheques for several thousands of pounds were passed through Mr. Hudson's account and found their way into the avaricious hands of Marks and his two collaborators. Very occasionally when a horse won the gang would pay Goudie half the winnings, but their information, of course, was deliberately bad so that the horses did not win and Marks and his fellow blackmailers got the entire bet.

It was an ingenious pattern of blackmail because although Goudie was in jeopardy the whole time the gang always had the protection of Marks' betting business. They could keep records which purported to show that Goudie was just another client.

In the end only Marks escaped. He went to France—and vanished. Burge and Mances were both convicted and sentenced to imprisonment and Goudie himself received ten years for his fantastic crime. The gang had appeared on the scene very early and Goudie had only enjoyed a few weeks of careless freedom. After that it had been hell, for he was always walking in the shadow of exposure, robbing his own bank not to enrich himself but to keep this sinister triumvirate satisfied.

Quite a lot of the money was recovered, not from Goudie, who was penniless, but from the gang who had invested it in government stock and bought houses for relatives. Marks had been in such a hurry to escape that he had had to leave a small fortune behind. At the trial at Liverpool Assizes Mr. F. E. Smith, who appeared for the prosecution, said: 'Perhaps no great embezzler has ever enjoyed so little of his robbery.' It may be that it was this that accounted for the sentence of ten years which might well conceivably, at this time, have been fifteen. With remission for good conduct which he earned, Goudie was released in seven years, so that at the time of his release he was still only thirty-six. He changed his name and secured modest employment and continued to attend race meetings, betting in very small amounts. The addiction had been cured.

The case of Thomas Peterson Goudie was a classic case of blackmail. Once the gang had ascertained the true facts, there was no way in which Goudie could escape the trap. The terror of exposure hung over him night and day. The three evil men were the masters of his destiny. It is a case that shows, better than most, how awful is the intimidation of ruthless blackmail.

The second case of blackmail which I wish to relate has none of the pathetic quality that surrounds the case of Goudie. Franz von Veltheim was an Austrian aristocrat of magnificent appearance. He was six foot, four inches tall, magnificently made, with fine, regular features, a very firm chin and two hard, grey eyes. He had a cruel mouth, but he was so good-looking, so gracious and often so gay that most people, women in particular, only saw the dashing debonair swagger of the man without having time to assess the less pleasing characteristics of his appearance.

Von Veltheim had always lived like a lord, or perhaps more accurately, like a millionaire. His main source of income was extracting money from women. He had quite extraordinary personal magnetism and during the course of a fairly long career he had managed to rob a large number of women, none of whom would give evidence against him, and many of whom insisted that he was the victim of circumstances and was not to blame for his manner of life. This in itself is a tribute to Von Veltheim's extraordinary powers. When he attended a glittering function he was immediately the centre of all eyes, much in the same way as the great Edwardian beauties were. We read of men standing on chairs to catch but a glimpse of Lily Langtry. Women would go to almost any lengths to engineer an introduction to this attractive, plausible and monstrous man.

It was no good the clubs of Europe blackballing Franz von Veltheim because they said he cheated at cards. The great hostesses did not believe it for a moment. It was jealousy on the part of the other men who were determined to injure him because of his great success. Von Veltheim, of course, made many enemies. More than half his conqests were married women and after they had been robbed, as well as ravished, their husbands often took a poor view of the charming aristocrat. In fact, von Veltheim was lucky to escape alive. It would not have been at all surprising if his body had been found floating in the Seine or in the Rhine with a bullet through his skull. He owed his survival to a wonderful sense of timing. He knew exactly when to vanish, never leaving it a day too late.

Von Veltheim was a confidence trickster as well as a blackmailer. He should never have come to England. He should have stuck to countries where romantic freebooters were rewarded, such as South Africa, then a new, dynamic and rumbustious place where his special talents could be put to good use. However, he had to leave South Africa. He managed to persuade a South African jury that he had not murdered Mr. Woolf Joel, but as soon as that unhappy incident was over he started to blackmail Mr. Solly Joel, who refused to be blackmailed and who visited England. Von Veltheim unwisely followed him. Now the Joel family had had to fight their way up in the rugged conditions of South African diamond-mining life and Woolf Joel had needed a capable and presentable 'front man' to help with him certain deals and negotiations. He thought that von Veltheim was just the man he needed. How wrong he was. The two men quarrelled and Woolf Joel died of a gunshot wound which the jury found was fired by von Veltheim in self-defence. This situation had led to von Veltheim knowing a great deal about confidential affairs of the Joel family. Hence the attempt to blackmail Solly Joel.

Scotland Yard was extremely well informed about Franz von Veltheim and their record showed that from 1883 he had lived a life of bigamy, blackmail, confidence tricking, forgery and cheating. But von Veltheim's description of his activities was entirely different. His account of his life in the period investigated showed him as an adventurous hero, the friend of princes, occasionally dogged by bad fortune but always coming up smiling, unconquerable, a man in a million.

The somewhat stolid detectives of Scotland Yard, used to taking statements from unimaginative British criminals, were stunned when von Veltheim dictated to them—it seemed inevitable that he should dictate—this wonderfully bizarre account of his life and activities.

'In 1883 I made a long trip, trying to join the Chinese in their fight against France, but arrived too late, for the French force had sunk the Chinese Navy at Fu-chow. During 1883–4 I travelled to China, Japan and Java, merely as an adventurer, and eventually found myself in England again, whence I returned to my native country, always travelling under the name of von Veltheim. After spending a few weeks with my relatives I became restless again, and started off in quest of new adventures. After travelling through Italy, I made my way down to the Mediterranean and crossed over to Algeria. On one occasion, having ventured into a wild and desolate district of the interior, I narrowly escaped capture by brigands, and for two days and nights was lost in the hill country, and only reached friendly shelter again with the greatest difficulty, in a famished and very exhausted condition. Algeria, although it was possible to obtain plenty of excitement there, did not offer a prospect of making much money, and as I was running short of funds I decided to return to Europe.

'I made the acquaintance of a neighbour and cousin of mine who was the Master of the Household of Prince Alexander of Bulgaria, who gave me an invitation to come out there. While there in the autumn of 1885, Roumania declared war on Bulgaria. The Emperor of Russia recalled his officers in the Bulgarian Army, which left them practically without any superior officers. At the time there were some nine or ten visitors—Germans, Austrians and English—who were on leave or who had been officers, who promptly offered their services to Prince Alexander.

'I became a personal friend of Prince Alexander—a most charming man and brave soldier, and was attached as a volunteer to his staff. My longing for active service in the battlefield was fully gratified, and I was in the thick of the fighting at Rirnova on November 24th, when I was slightly wounded, and at Pierrot five days later, when I received a much more serious wound, and, much to my disgust, had to be invalided to Bucharest. By the time I had sufficiently recovered to take part in active service again the war was over, so it was necessary to look for a new field of adventure.'

This fantastic tale, all of it untrue, was more cunning than it would appear to be today. Emperors and princes were at that time regarded by the general public not only with respect but with awe. In Paris, in Rome, and in London society was quite small and its doors were not easily unlocked. Members of these close coteries tended to move in a world apart, like the old English lady who, when her daughter returned from Italy, greeted her with the words: 'And tell me, dear, how is the good queen?' So von Veltheim's fabrications were calculated to impress and as nearly all the characters he mentions had died it was very difficult to disprove his story directly. However, the South African police had a very extensive dossier on von Veltheim which they supplied to Scotland Yard, so that when the fairy-tale was being told the real facts were already in the possession of the detectives taking the statement. It was an ominous situation for the adventurer.

There was no end to the ingenuity of this attractive rogue. He invented a story of a close friendship with the Boer leader Paul Kruger, who was said to have hidden a vast treasure when hunted by the all-conquering British. Von Veltheim estimated the treasure at ten million pounds sterling and raised quite large sums of money to finance an expedition to recover it. The snag, of course, being that the treasure did not exist.

However, the incurable confidence trickster would probably have survived until age had ravaged his handsome appearance had he not, most unwisely, blackmailed Mr. Solly Joel. Now Mr. Solly Joel liked Britain and British ways and British racing and he acquired a number of British habits, including a resolute refusal to be blackmailed. Von Veltheim had not expected this. In the different climate of South Africa all such matters could be arranged, but not in Britain, which, at this time, was a very black and white country.

So the end of the story for this dazzling bird of paradise was the Old Bailey. Von Veltheim was unlucky on two counts. First of all his judge was Mr. Justice Phillimore, who had an absolute phobia about immorality, who regarded women as being semi-divine and therefore thought that men who took advantage of womanly weakness were savage human beasts. Secondly, Sir Charles Gill led for the Crown in this case, and Sir Charles Gill, when he was convinced of a man's guilt, could be a mordant and terrifying master of cross-examination. Sir Charles asked why all the persons referred to by von Veltheim were dead? Von Veltheim, still full of fight, said that presumably this was due to acts of God for which he could not really be held responsible. This was a very good answer, but Sir Charles was tenacious, pursuing the matter until he forced the prisoner to suggest that he had explanations but that to give them would involve a breach of confidence with the very highest of the land. Now this was the misty land of fabrication in which rogues like to travel and at the end of the long and deadly cross-examination von Veltheim seemed a very much smaller man. He had entered the dock with the air of a medieval knight unaccountably arrested by a race of pygmies who wanted to put questions to him. He was still beautifully dressed, with exquisite manners and a delightfully sardonic turn of wit. It was almost painful to see this rare being cut down by the insistent probing questions of the lawyer, but cut down he was until he visibly shrank and looked older than his age instead of considerably younger, as was his wont.

Von Veltheim himself, when he was depressed about the case, thought that he might, if he was unlucky, be convicted and sentenced, perhaps, to five years' imprisonment. What actually happened was that the judge passed on him what must surely be regarded as one of the most savage sentences of the twentieth century. In quiet conversational tones Mr. Justice Phillimore said: 'You have rightly been convicted of this abominable crime and for years have lived a life of duplicity and merciless extortion. I sentence you to twenty years' imprisonment.'

To von Veltheim this was a death sentence. He collapsed when he heard it.

I am glad to say that the Home Secretary corrected the terrible sentence, reducing it to fifteen years. During the war von Veltheim was transferred to an internment camp and later deported to his native country. As recently as 1923 he was in trouble again in South Africa, but he was growing old now, the flair had departed. The grand days were over. Never again would this meteor of a man blaze his way to riches by his extraordinary gifts and through the vulnerability and weakness of his victims.

9

Charley Lester and his *Naklengs*

CHARLEY LESTER was an implacable intimidator. He made his living for twenty years by frightening people in Siam. His story is an unusual one, for Charley Lester was an Englishman, and it is uncommon for Englishmen to become gangsters in the Far East, where formerly the British and the French were the paramount powers. But that overlordship never applied to Siam and it was this that gave Charley Lester his chance that he seized in both his muscular hands, pressing the orange until the pips squeaked.

It all happened in the days of good King Mongkut who was the absolute ruler of Siam. This was the time when Anna Leonowens was teaching the royal children and especially the king's eldest son, Chow Fa Chulalongkorn, who was to become one of the wisest and most modern-minded monarchs that Siam has ever seen.

In King Mongkut's day liberalism, in the modern sense, had not arrived in Siam. Slavery was on the way out, but was not abolished legally until the young King Chulalongkorn took over. Everyone knelt in the presence of the king, and sons knelt in the presence of their fathers. It was a conservative country. Not the intellectual conservatism of Mr. Nixon, Lord Butler or Mr. Heath, but the natural and divine conservatism of Charles II.

Charley Lester arrived in Siam on the British S.S. *Sir William Hardwick*. He was third mate. The S.S. *Sir William Hardwick* was eight thousand tons and this enabled her to pass over the bar at Paknam and, with a pilot on board, make the fifteen miles to Bangkok, keeping midstream on the great winding brown river, the Menam Chow Phya.

G

As the ship rounded the last bend on the river, Charley was on the bridge with Captain Anderson and through his binoculars he caught his first sight of the Siamese capital. He never forgot it. Dominating the scene was the Grand Palace, with its white castellated walls that appeared to be a city within a city. Its multi-coloured temples shone and sparkled in the sunlight of a clear blue sky. It was December and the heat of the long summer—as well as the rains—was over. The temperature still shot up to the middle seventies or even eighty during the noon hours, but the mornings were lovely, fresh and cool, and the nights were a velvet dream lighted by the stars that seemed bigger and more lustrous than Charley—who had travelled a good deal for a young man—had ever seen before.

Charley was twenty-seven. He was a formidable figure for so young a man. He gave the impression that he might have had some years in the boxing ring and, in fact, he had tried his hand at professional boxing before he turned to the sea. He had red hair that grew *en brosse*. His eyes were blue and hard, merciless eyes that one did not notice when he was laughing or smiling, as he often was. He had ears that stood out from his head and he moved most unexpectedly like a cat, quickly, quietly, with no effort at all.

Charley was a young man who noticed what was going on. On board the *Sir William Hardwick* there was a young Siamese prince, a cousin of the king's, returning with his entourage from London where he had been learning English and engineering. Charley Lester noticed that all the Siamese knelt when the prince spoke to them and seemed highly honoured that he should address them at all. Charley's deduction from this was that perhaps a determined man could become a leader in Siam, even if he was a foreigner.

The Siamese Government at this time employed a fairly large number of foreigners, mainly in the police force. Siamese were being trained, of course, to take over all the positions in government, but the situation was such that it looked as if foreigners would be employed in various capacities for many years. The nations who supplied the foreign government servants were Britain and Denmark, both countries having a long history of association with Siam. America had not yet appeared on the scene, except for her missionaries, who found it impossible to convert the Siamese from their staunchly held Buddhist faith, but whose doctors were greatly welcomed by the people in the country districts who were beginning to lose faith in their astrologers, diviners and medicine men who practised the old arts of healing in Siam.

Charley had been signed on as third mate of the *Sir William Hardwick* at the last moment as a replacement for a Welshman who had gone sick with ulcer trouble. Captain Anderson quite liked him, but secretly did not trust him. He had an idea that Charley was making the trip to secure a free passage to the Far East where he might well desert the ship if he thought that opportunity was knocking on his door. He was dead right. This was exactly what Charley Lester did do.

When the *Sir William Hardwick,* its Blue Peter flying, was ready to up-anchor and sail downriver for the open sea, Charley was nowhere to be seen. Captain Anderson realised at once what had happened, muttered, 'The bastard,' and gave orders for his ship to sail.

Captain Anderson knew it was hopeless to find Charley Lester if he had gone underground in one of the teeming native markets of the city, probably with a girl. They had tried to recapture a runaway seaman on a previous trip and had wasted a whole day and missed the tide as a result. Charley Lester had, in fact, not wasted his time. True, he had joined up with a Siamese girl, but not the kind of girl Captain Anderson had in mind. He had met Meilai in the office of her father, Colonel Srivieng, who was a Siamese colonel of police. Meilai thought she read a message in those hard blue eyes of the tall Englishman, and she was not mistaken.

The colonel had been helpful. 'So you want a job with our police? You are British. You have not been convicted of any crime. You are twenty-seven and physically fit. You may do. We lost a young officer yesterday of the cholera. Come with me. I take you to Colonel Brownwell.'

Colonel Brownwell was the British assistant chief of police. The chief of police was Mom Rachawongse Apaiwongse, an able and energetic Siamese prince but recently arrived from Europe. Colonel Brownwell ran the day-to-day business of the force. He hired and he fired.

Colonel Srivieng knocked at a door, saluted and said to the burly figure seated behind a massive teak desk, 'Young man. British. Twenty-seven. No record, wishes to join us.'

Colonel Brownwell looked up from the letters he was signing and said, 'Please be seated.' He finished signing the letters, rang a bell, handed the letters to a sergeant who entered the room, and then turned his attention to Charley Lester. He scrutinised him for perhaps a minute, but to Charley it seemed very much longer. Colonel Brownwell, who was experienced in men, decided that there was a chance that Charley would make a good policeman, decisive, determined, probably brave and certainly intelligent. He thought that there was also a chance that Charley would exploit the peculiar temptations to which the Siamese police were subject at this time. But that poor young man had died yesterday and they were very short of capable officers. . . .

'Right. We'll take you. You understand this is a Siamese service, subject to the orders of the Siamese authorities?'

'Yes, sir.'

'Your pay will be eighty baht a month to start with. You will sign a service contract initially for three years. You will go now for three months to our officer training school. Then you will be commissioned as a second-lieutenant and probably serve in one of the police stations in Bangkok, though you may be posted up-country at any time—to Chiengmai or Songkla, for instance. Is that clear?'

'Yes, Sir. Thank you.'

The colonel shook hands with his new recruit and Charley was on his way.

Charley Lester should have contacted his ship to tell Captain Anderson that he was staying in Siam, but Charley had an idea that if he did this Captain Anderson might arrest him, as indeed he could have done. So when the sailing of the S.S. *Sir William Hardwick* was reported in the *Bangkok Observer,* Charley breathed a sigh of relief. His old life was off. His new life was on.

Now the thoughts that had passed through Charley's mind during the interview with Colonel Brownwell were quite different from the speculations that had been animating the colonel. Charley, during the week that the *Sir William Hardwick* had been in port, had come to certain conclusions about Siam.

These conclusions were first that the girls were lovely and that Charley's brand of hard and rugged manhood attracted them instantly. The second conclusion was that Siam was completely 'unspoilt'. Everything in the market was very cheap indeed. One could buy fifty delicious *pla tu* (mackerel) for five satangs, about three pence. The tical was ten to the pound—two shillings—and one could live in comparative luxury on a tical a day. True, the eighty baht a month starting salary in the police was very small, but then Charley would be kept and given a house and garden and one servant—free. Moreover, after his first year, his salary nearly doubled to one hundred and fifty baht a month, which was riches. The third conclusion that Charley had very much in mind was that the police force in Siam at this time, if one kept in with the right people, offered opportunities for making money that made the official salary comparatively unimportant.

Nothing had been said by Colonel Brownwell on the subject of Charley learning Siamese. Much of the office work was in fact done at this time in English, but Charley saw at once that he must speak Siamese fluently to exploit the many situations that might arise. So Meilai taught him the Thai tongue. This was a great advantage because it meant that he did not speak the common language of the market place but learnt the Siamese used by the ruling families in Siam, with all the various changes of words and inflection that signified whether the person addressed was a superior, an equal, or an inferior. His mastery of Siamese stood Charley in good stead. He could not possibly have achieved what he did achieve without it.

He was grateful to Meilai and after he had been commissioned he asked her father's permission to marry her. At first this was refused on the grounds that 'Siamese ladies never marry foreigners'. But under pressure from his daughter the colonel relented and the couple were married according to Siamese custom before a chapter of saffron-robed priests, the silver cord knotting together one to the other in symbolic union. Charley did not think it worth while registering this marriage with the British Embassy. He preferred to remain unmarried as far as the British were concerned. Charley Lester always kept his options open.

So, within a matter of months, Charley Lester had penetrated the world of the Siamese both officially and socially. It was a world of power, for the Siamese had complete control of their army, their Civil Service, and their police, but it was a world that the foreign merchants and even the foreign embassies often knew very little about. The foreign business men carried on their trade through Chinese *compradores* and these were the men who had contact with the markets and the people. The embassies held 'bridge' parties with the idea of bringing the embassy staff into social contact with Siamese officials, but these efforts very seldom resulted in the formation of any friendship or any intimacy between the embassies and the Siamese. Charley, on the other hand, had passed through the silken curtain. He was living on the Siamese side of the fence. He realised that to some extent this would cut him off from the young men in the trading firms who played rugger, and polo and the eternal game of chasing the 'Mems', the white married women. But Charley did not mind this. He 'had one simple aim and ambition—to get rich quick and then get out.

Charley Lester was appointed as junior officer in Bangrak police station and he was a diligent and quick learner in the policeman's profession. He learned police routine as it existed in Siam, he learned a great deal concerning the Siamese underworld and the curious people described as 'naklengs' by the Siamese public. It was almost a calling to be a *nakleng*. The first rule of a *nakleng's* life was that he never, if he could help it, did any honest work. He regarded it as beneath his dignity. Work was for slaves and the dumb ones.

Naklengs lived from gambling, burglary, blackmail, extortion and women. They had a strange habit of dressing with great flamboyance—it was almost a uniform. They would wear orange shirts and blue 'Chinese' trousers and vivid floppy hats that protected them from the sun. They had not yet taken to dark glasses that later were to be almost a monopoly of the *naklengs*.

Charley Lester saw that quite a number of *naklengs* were also police informers, and very valuable informers too. After all, the *naklengs* and the police were in the same business, though their approach to it was substantially different. It occurred to Charley Lester very early in his career that a combination of *naklengs* led by a police officer in a secure position—trusted by his superiors—would be a most powerful union. He bore this very much in mind for the future.

Then, suddenly, one day he was posted for a year to Chiengmai, the entrancing little northern capital of Siam.

At first this upset Charley very much. He was beginning to set up valuable contacts in Bangkok and he did not want them interrupted. But, on thinking the matter over, he decided to accept the transfer with good grace. It was not for long and it might even be an advantage to have contacts in the north, because the north was where the opium came from to be shipped down river, taking four weeks to reach Bangkok and the world markets. Opium was wealth. Much of the trade was, of course, legitimate. It was opium designed to become morphine and other derivatives for the open and legal pharmaceutical business of the world. But a substantial part of the trade was outside the law, and it was from this 'unofficial' opium that fortunes might be made.

The police were much concerned in the opium business. It was their duty to suppress it, but the temptations were great. If illicit opium was seized the fine imposed by the Siamese courts was four times the value of the opium and these fines were always promptly paid. They were a calculated business risk. It was obvious that a dealer in the illicit market would be prepared to pay handsomely to avoid a fine. And there was another aspect. Confiscated opium was seized by the police and it did not always find its way to the government go-downs in Bangkok. . . .

On the whole Charley Lester thought there might be compensations for spending a year in Chiengmai with Meilai. One of the compensations was that during the year he was promoted police captain and so had far greater authority than he had exercised up to now. He obtained a salary increase in addition and the house the ministry gave him near the river in Chiengmai was charming, built of teak, but cool and spacious, with a garden that sparkled with frangipani and hibiscus and the herbs that Meilai grew to flavour her curries.

Police Captain Lester was a very discreet officer. He never forgot to visit his superiors, the governor, the chief of Chiengmai Police, and one or two of the local princes, with presents and flowers on the occasion of the New Year, which at this time was held on the first of April. Their birthdays he also remembered. And Meilai helped him in his career. She was an attractive girl, tall for a Siamese, with that instantaneous gaiety and spontaneity that seem to bless some of the children of the sunshine. The official wives liked her. She never ran after their husbands and she was always ready to play a session of cards on one of the broad verandahs of their houses. When she won she was grateful, and when she lost she just smiled and said she had enjoyed her visit so very much.

Charley's work centred on the old police station that was halfway between the town and the little golf-course which some of the Europeans in the teak firms had just built. But quite often Charley's work took him into the Laos country to the north, or even as far as Muang Fang towards Burma. The Prince of Chiengmai was married to a cousin of the King of Ava in Mandalay and there was quite a lot of commerce between Siam and Burma by the northern routes, mainly by elephant, but also by mule and Shan pony and on foot.

Charley studied the opium situation very carefully. He wanted to get rich, but he did not want, on any account, to lose his job. Chiengmai seemed fairly safe. The officials were mainly elderly and very traditional. That is to say they thought it natural for a man to supplement his government salary with such presents as might come his way. This being the climate, Charley Lester began to organise.

He found that with very little effort on his part he acquired two henchmen. One was a Thai, Nai Tuan, a thin cadaverous man who smoked opium in moderation, a habit rare among the Thais. The other was Chieng Lee, a fat Chinese who lived by his wits—and contrived to live quite well. Both these men attached themselves to Captain Lester and became that curious mixture of friend, servant, bodyguard and retainer that was instantly recognisable in the East but for which there was no counterpart in the West.

Charley Lester's first big coup was to seize nearly a hundredweight of illicit opium in the possession of Chow Krasit. Now Chow Krasit was, of course, a relative of the Prince of Chiengmai, therefore Charley had to move carefully. He did not want to make powerful enemies. So he merely confiscated the drug—and waited. No words were spoken, but the move was understood. Meilai, three days later, was asked to play cards at the house of Chow Krasit's wife and on opening her handbag when she returned home she found ten thousand ticals in one-hundred-tical notes carefully folded and placed in a pocket of the handbag. She gave the money to her husband. She did not discuss the matter with him. She knew and Charley knew that she knew that this was the release money for the confiscated opium. It was duly returned and the record was marked: 'Legal drug wrongly seized in transit.' This was a smooth operation. There had been no letters, no notes, no words, no agreement, no discussion. Yet everyone had perfectly understood the situation. At the next New Year Charley presented Chow Krasit with a gong made of ivory with gold trimmings. It was the traditional gift of friendship and respect.

But not all Charley Lester's extra-mural activities went as happily as this one. He had been in Chiengmai six months, half his period of service in the north, when a rival gang—if you will pardon the expression—closed in on Charley Lester, and Charley realised to his great discomfort that he was being blackmailed. The leader of the opposition, as it were, was a rich Chinese merchant who dealt in teak, sapphires, rubies (from the mines near the Burma border) and, needless to say, opium.

His name was Ah Wongse and the proposition that he put to Charley Lester was partnership or—Charley did not like this at all. He realised that Ah Wongse knew of all his activities and could make up a dossier that would probably lead to Charley being dismissed from the police force. Charley summoned Nai Tuan and Chieng Lee and said: 'The Chinaman Ah Wongse is trying to injure me. I want him to suffer and be scared for his life. Arrange it.'

So the following week Ah Wogse was kidnapped from his place of business by masked men who took him outside the town and beat him. He was then given a message: 'If you try to injure Police Captain Lester you will die.'

He was then released and had to walk six miles through the jungle to reach the comparative safety of his home.

Ah Wongse thought the matter over. If he did inform on Charley Lester the complaint would probably be forwarded to the Ministry of Interior in Bangkok. It might be weeks before action was taken and long before that time Ah Wongse would be a corpse floating down the Mei Ping. He did not like the idea. He decided to drop the blackmail project and he steered very clear of Charley Lester for the remainder of his tour in the north.

After this Charley met with more than modest success. The underworld of the illicit opium trade recognised that here was a police officer not to be trifled with, a man capable of hitting back if he was attacked.

Charley had many profitable incidents. There was that great moment when he and his men stopped a convoy of elephants, loaded with opium, making their way to Chiengmai by the river route. Charley took the lot quietly and sold it discreetly. He captured the guards and mahouts, but, after terrifying them, let them go. No police record of the seizure was ever made.

Yet Charley kept up his official reputation. Many smaller seizures of the drug stood to his credit and on the king's birthday he was actually given a medal by the government 'in recognition of his diligent enforcement of the law against smuggling and contraband'.

As the governor pinned the medal to his uniform not a flicker of a smile crossed the young man's face. There was a time and a place for laughter, but this was not one of them. He saluted smartly and gravely and Meilai took his photograph looking very handsome—and resolute—with the new medal pinned to his tunic.

When Charley's time in Chiengmai was up he returned to Bangkok and was given the command of his old station, Bangrak. He had had a good year. His reputation in the force remained high—and he had made ten thousand pounds sterling. He was careful not to send the money to a European bank. The European bankers were not discreet. He sent the money by a Chinese bank to Hong Kong and from there it was sent to London in Meilai's name.

Charley Lester planned to spend four more years in Siam. His contract was renewed after three years for a further two years. He was promoted police major, a rapid promotion. Nai Tuan and Chieng Lee accompanied their master to the great city. They had been well rewarded for their co-operation and loyalty and were now joined by six additional men of menace.

In Bangkok, Charley Lester was soon operating on a much bigger scale. He and his *naklengs* had a virtual monopoly of the river route by which the illicit opium reached Bangkok and the open sea. Charley was now considered by his superiors to know all the tricks of the opium trade (as indeed he did), for had he not served a year in Chiengmai where the sticky, odoriferous black gold came from? So he was put in charge of counter-contraband operations. This gave him new opportunities on a much bigger scale. He found that in Bangkok he had to establish a reputation for toughness as he had done in Chiengmai. He rapidly did so. His enemies were invariably beaten up and told that one more step out of turn and they would die. They invariably took the hint. They did not want to die at the hands of Nai Tuan and Chieng Lee, who were said to have some novel ways of procuring a slow death so that (a) the victim knew that he was dying and (b) there was nothing whatever he could do about it.

It is to the eternal credit of Charley Lester that he never actually murdered anyone. The treatment that Nai Tuan and Chieng Lee handed out to their master's enemies, plus their direct and simple threat of death, was always sufficient.

At the end of his five years in Siam, Charley decided that his luck had held long enough. He had eighty thousand pounds invested in banks and stock in the city of London, equivalent perhaps to a million pounds today. Charley had a feeling that it could not go on. Besides, the king had become perturbed by rumours that his police force was more corrupt than was customary. So he appointed a relation, Mom Chow Kritabutra, as chief of police with orders to 'clean up the police'. The prince had been trained as a policeman in England and in the States and Charley Lester thought he saw a dark and dangerous cloud on the horizon. He resigned, to the great regret of his superiors. Meilai and Charley were festooned with garlands as they boarded their ship for Singapore and London. They had a great send-off.

Charley bought a farm of about two hundred acres and turned gentleman farmer. They had many visitors from Siam and Meilai loved to entertain the Siamese who had made the pilgrimage out to the Lesters' place. Meilai returned to visit her relatives for the winter every three years. She would have liked Charley to go with her, but he only smiled and said: 'No. You go and come back to me soon.' That she did, for she had learned to love the man.

When curious neighbours asked how Major Lester had made his pile in the East, the answer always was: 'In tea, I believe.'

But at this time no tea was grown in Siam. It was another crop, the white poppy, that made men rich. The stuff that dreams are made of, and Charley, looking back now on his five years in Siam, could hardly believe it had really happened.

There was a great shake-up in the force the year after Charley left. Heads rolled, and Charley realised that his timing had been perfect.

Charley settled down completely. He detested the idea of any kind of adventure. All he wanted was his farm, his house, his very comfortable income—and Meilai.

He knew that the gods had smiled upon him.

10

Paul Jones

O N the 14th of July 1747, in the Stewartry of Kirkoudbright
in Scotland, John Paul, a gardener, had a son his wife
bore him after a short labour. The boy was known as John
Paul like his father, but, while he was still a young man, he
added the name Jones and became Paul Jones, a name which
became famous in America and infamous in Britain, and
which is not forgotten even to this day.

Paul Jones, as we shall now call him, was a most unlikely
son for a gardener to have. It is true that for few a years he
followed in his father's footsteps, doing the humbler chores of
the gardener's vocation, literally grubbing weeds from garden
paths with a broken dinner knife. He was only educated in the
parish school and had no further education, but such was the
discipline of eighteenth-century teaching in Scotland that he
could read and write quite well and could add and subtract—
especially add—reasonably well. As it turned out, this was all
the education he needed for the fantastic career which he was
to pursue. Of course, he had other qualities which made up
for his educational deficiencies. Even as a boy he felt the lure
of the sea and concocted elaborate and extraordinary schemes
for making money in the American trade, both legitimately
and illegitimately. Above and beyond all this Paul Jones was
courageous, unscrupulous, inventive and had a compelling
presence, possessing those qualities which later were to
induce men to follow his lead wherever he went.

Paul Jones was lucky in the age into which he was born.
The British still ruled the American colonies from Whitehall
but the turbulent and independent spirit of the British
settlers was already moving towards political independence of

Britain. That independence was only prevented from including Canada by the defeat of the French armies which sought to establish a French empire in northern America. The period was a type of interregnum in which neither the law of Britain nor any other law was completely effective. It was an open invitation to bold and bad men to make their fortunes quickly and this they did, provided they were ruthless enough and were fortunate in escaping arrest, imprisonment or death by hanging.

Paul Jones appears to have started his speculations in contraband while he was still in his teens, but he almost certainly became an apprentice to a merchant in the American trade, making long voyages between Europe and America. During this time he lost the small fortune he had acquired while he was still very young and he lost it because the British authorities caught up with him, fining him and impounding the contraband. They were never able to arrest him, but at least they could ruin him. There is no doubt that for the rest of his life he bore an implacable grudge against his own country and this decided him to join the American rebels and led to one of the strangest adventures ever achieved by a renegade. Paul Jones was to emerge as a truly great intimidator, for, as he grew in cunning, daring and ferocity, people whispered his name in fear and men were very careful not to cross his path lest his vengeance fall on them.

With this background it is not surprising that when the American colonists decided to retaliate against the English by building a fleet of their own one of their earliest and most eager recruits should be the seaman, Paul Jones. On the 22nd December 1775 he was made a lieutenant in the American Navy which during that year began its history.

We must record that the early history of the American Navy was chaotic. The ferocious discipline which stamped the British Navy did not exist. Officers and men fraternised freely and it was fortunate if an order was instantly obeyed. Nearly all the seamen of the new fleet got drunk as often as they could and it was their habit to bring their women on board their ships when in harbour. The American Navy had very few gunnery experts and the primitive weapons of the time were apt to explode on board instead of directing themselves at the enemy. This being the general situation, it was not surprising that the first ventures in which Paul Jones took part met with a marked lack of success.

The American fleet was ordered to take New Providence, one of the Bahama islands, but British intelligence learnt of the matter and they met with such stiff opposition that they had to withdraw. As they were in the process of withdrawing, a single powerful British man-of-war iflnicted great damage on the fleet. It is an incident that naturally does not appear in the history books of the United States, nor, for that matter, in the history books of Britain, to whom it was a very minor episode.

An inquiry was ordered into this naval fiasco with the object of finding out first why the fleet had not taken New Providence by surprise, and, secondly, why a single British man-of-war, however powerful, had been able to inflict heavy damage on the American fleet.The result of the official enquiry showed that only one man had acted with any sense of direction and command and that was Paul Jones. It became clear during the enquiry that Paul Jones had a knowledge of naval tactics and strategy which most of his superiors did not pretend to possess. Moreover, he had shown exceptional courage and presence of mind in action. His talents were rewarded by promotion and by a gift of money.

There is no doubt that Paul Jones, if he had had a free hand, could have built up an American Navy of efficiency and power. However, there were still officers of senior rank, American, French and Dutch by nationality, and they had no intention of allowing Paul Jones to jump the gun of promotion any more than he had already done. In 1776 Congress fitted out fifteen frigates, but Paul Jones did not get a command which he would dearly have loved to have been given.

It looked at this point as if the hierarchy were never going to allow Paul Jones to control a major naval exercise or escapade, but clearly the powers that ruled in the new confederacy valued his advice, for we find him writing letters to the Honourable Mr. Morris, the Minister in Charge of

Naval Affairs, in which he said: 'It is folly to pretend to scorn the navy of England, which is the best regulated navy in the world. We may take their navy as our pattern and aim at such further improvements as may one day make ours vie with and exceed theirs.'

However, Paul Jones had his successes. During the year 1776 he destroyed eight English ships and took eight captive. Towards the end of this year he saw action while sailing with the *Providence,* a sloop with twelve six-pounders. The *Providence* was accompanied by two more powerful ships, the *Solebay* with twenty-three guns and the *Mitford* with thirty-two guns. He recovered his health, which he had lost through an attack of pneumonia, and was at last given a captain's commission. He was put in charge of a squadron in Rhode Island with the idea of attacking Isle Royal. While he was engaged in this enterprise he captured the *Mellish,* an armed merchantman from Liverpool. This was a very useful windfall, for the *Mellish* was carrying ten thousand suits of uniform intended for General Burgoyne's army. As Washington's army at this moment had no military clothing, the uniforms (with a little alteration) came in extremely useful.

It was no longer possible for the fraternity of the officers of the American Navy to keep Paul Jones from the highest positions. His rank was now official and formalised. He was regarded as an American and he was undoubtedly the most daring and capable American naval commander. In Whitehall, of course, a different view was taken of him. He was a traitor, having levied war against the King of England, and he was a pirate who had robbed peaceful merchantmen on the high seas. He had also murdered quite a number of people. Treason, murder and piracy were the three major offences in the English criminal calendar. A man convicted of treason or of murder or of piracy was automatically hanged by the neck until he was dead. He was also drawn and quartered, often after death, but sometimes as he was dying from strangulation. His quartered carcass was then exhibited in various public places and his head was allowed to rot on a pike in some prominent place where the public could see it. The flesh was soaked in aniseed so that the birds would not be

H

likely to consume it, the general idea being that the rotting flesh would suggest to the people at large that it was dangerous to indulge in treason, murder or piracy. So we have Paul Jones a trusted hero on one side of the Atlantic and a despised and dreaded public enemy on the other. It was a situation which would have caused most men to hesitate and to think again before they continued in the service of the sea.

The commanders of the American Navy in the year 1777 decided that 'as a reward for the zeal he had shown, and for the signal services which he had performed with little force' Paul Jones should be sent to the American commissioners in Paris and that they should invest him with the command of the finest ship that could be obtained.

It is extraordinary that Paul Jones did not fall in with this suggestion and yet it is typical of him that he should have made a counter-suggestion. He sent a letter to the secret committees putting forward a new plan. This extraordinary proposal was that he should be sent to Europe to attack the coasts of England. After the committee had recovered from their initial shock at this seemingly outrageous proposal they decided that a man who was fearless enough to suggest it might well be intrepid enough to carry it out.

The object of the attacks on the English coasts was, of course, in Paul Jones's own words, to show 'that not all their boasted navy can protect their own coasts, and that the scenes of distress which they have occasioned in America may soon be brought home to their own doors'.

So it was that Paul Jones sailed to France, hoisting his Union flag of thirteen stars, white in a blue field. He had the honour of the first salute which the American flag ever received from a foreign power. The Conte D'Orvilliers, the French naval commander, saluted the Union flag as it sailed into Brest.

Paul Jones had his plans already fully formulated in his agile mind. Knowing that secrecy was essential to surprise, which in its turn was essential to success, he kept his own counsel, but, in fact, he had decided 'to descend upon Whitehaven'. It should be noted here, I think, that his commission had been to attack the coasts of England. Paul

Jones interpreted this as meaning that he could land men on the coast, burn a few villages, and get away in the confusion. It was a liberal interpretation of his instructions.

On the 10th April 1778 he sailed from Brest. Neither wind nor weather was favourable, but he tacked laboriously up the Channel, sinking any vessels in sight to prevent news of his coming reaching the mainland. There is no evidence that he bothered to pick up survivors.

On the 22nd of April he arrived off Whitehaven. The weather was calm and it was the lightest of winds that brought the *Ranger* to within a quarter of a mile of the shore. Now Whitehaven was a town of some fifty thousand inhabitants and there were nearly two hundred ships in the harbour. The town was protected by a great wall and it was a plan of the utmost daring to row ashore silently and secretly at night a handful of men with gunpowder and guns, and to create such havoc and promote such chaos that, by dawn, great damage would be inflicted in the material sense on the sleeping British and, of course, even greater psychological damage to the nation as a whole, but this was the enterprise that Paul Jones had planned, and this was the enterprise which, as we shall see, he largely carried out.

The tides caused a delay that might have been fatal to a less resolute leader than Paul Jones. The day had dawned before his men reached land, but he carried on. He sent Lieutenant Wallingford with the combustibles to the north side of the harbour to fire the ships anchored there, while he himself led his men in scaling the walls. They surprised and secured the sentinels and locked them up in the guard-house. The party then spiked the guns of all the cannon in the south fort. At this moment there was a desperate anxiety. Why had the party with the combustibles not done their work? Why were the British ships in the harbour not already ablaze? Paul Jones, who was a firm believer in the axiom that if you want a thing done with despatch you have to do it yourself, raced round with his party to find out what had happened. The light that was to have fused the combustibles had become extinguished and the party was dithering, uncertain what to do. Paul Jones immediately secured another light from a house by the harbour and soon a British ship anchored alongside was blazing, the flames nourished with barrels of tar. Moreover, the flames were spreading to the nearby vessels.

It is interesting to note that Paul Jones was one of the early exploiters of the hi-jack technique. He took three of the sentinels prisoner and put them aboard the *Ranger* as hostages. By this time the town and fortress of Whitehaven was in tumult. The army were rushing to the south fort to man their guns and sink the vessel of this impudent pirate whose ship was lying in the bay. Their fury and alarm when they found that all their cannon had been spiked can be imagined. It was more than an hour before fresh armour was trundled up and then it was not effective, the fusillade falling short of the *Ranger,* which, by that time, was sailing away on the tide.

Paul Jones's extraordinary attack on an important English naval town which was heavily fortified shook the whole country. Captain Johnson describes the reaction of the country in these words, writing just after the news had been received:

'The news of the descent traversed the country with the speed of the wind: all England was struck with amazement and terror. Every measure of defence was adopted that fear of instant invasion could suggest. Meetings were held, companies formed by subscriptions; strangers arrested; look-out vessels stationed at every port; forts everywhere repaired, and guns made ready for service. Paul Jones made the English feel in their own homes the dreadful evils of the war they were so eagerly carrying to the shores of another country. Wild and extravagant as the project might seem at first, to the resolute bravery of our hero its execution was easy. That their own coasts were open to attack, that a small part of a single ship's crew would attempt in a couple of open boats the destruction of a town and its whole harbour of shipping, were ideas that had not, and there is but a bare possibility that they could have, entered into the heads of our country-men. The fact once known, however, they were all activity and watchfulness.'

I think it is safe to assume that any other leader of an expedition of this kind would certainly not have struck twice in the same neighbourhood, but Paul Jones had conceived the idea of capturing the Earl of Selkirk who lived on the neighbouring St. Mary's Isle. Luckily for the earl, he had left for London on the previous day. The countess, however, was at home and it was only with the greatest difficulty that Paul Jones restrained his men from looting the whole house. After all, they said, the British kill and plunder in America, why should we not kill and plunder here? Paul Jones harangued his unruly crew, explaining to them that it was not possible or seemly for rude sailors to intrude into the home of the English nobility. What they thought of this exhortation coming from their leader is not recorded. However, as usual, Paul Jones had his way but he had to compromise and the whole very valuable collection of family plate of the house of Douglas was removed and put aboard the *Ranger*.

On the 8th of May 1788, writing from Brest and still aboard the *Ranger,* Paul Jones wrote a remarkable letter to the countess. It is apparently directed to persuading the countess to enlist her husband in the ranks of those who wanted to bring an end to the American war. The literary style of Paul Jones shows quite clearly his Scots upbringing and his American allegiance. It also reflects his profound respect for rank and title. I quote the concluding paragraphs of this gem of a letter:

'As the feelings of your gentle bosom cannot but be congenial with mine, let me entreat you, Madam, to use your persuasive art with your husband, to endeavour to stop this cruel and destructive war, in which Britain can never succeed. Heaven can never countenance the barbarous an unmanly practice of the Britons in America, which savages would blush at, and which, if not discontinued, will soon be retaliated on Britain by a justly enraged people. Should you fail in this (for I am persuaded that you will undertake it: and who can resist the power of such an advocate?) your endeavours to effect a general exchange of prisoners will be an act of humanity, which will afford you golden feelings on a death-bed.

'I hope this cruel contest will soon be closed; but should it continue, I wage no war with the fair. I acknowledge their force, and bend before it with submission. Let not, therefore, the amiable Countess of Selkirk regard me as an enemy: I am ambitious of her esteem and friendship, and would do any-thing, consistent with my duty, to merit it.

'The honour of a line from your hand, in answer to this, will lay me under a singular obligation; and if I can render you any acceptable service in France or elsewhere, I hope you see into my character so far as to command me without the least grain of reserve.

'I wish to know exactly the behaviour of my people, as I am determined to punish them if they have exceeded their liberty. I have the honour to be, with much esteem and with profound respect, Madam, &c. &c.

'John Paul Jones
'To the Countess of Selkirk.'

The curious end of this gallant correspondence was that Congress, at the instigation of Paul Jones, ordered the plate to be returned to the earl. Such were the vicissitudes of eighteenth-century warfare.

While the *Ranger* was hovering ominously outside St. Mary's Isle, Paul Jones could see the British ship *Drake* with some smaller vessels preparing for action. The tides were adverse to the *Drake* and prevented her coming within distance of the *Ranger*. However, *Ranger* did not sail off but waited for the tide to turn. When *Drake* was within hailing distance she sent up a signal demanding to know the name and nationality of the *Ranger*. The reply was somewhat unexpected. 'This is the American ship *Ranger*. We wait for you, and desire that you will come on; the sun is now little more than one hour from setting, it is therefore time to begin.' The action was described as hot, close and obstinate. The rigging of the *Drake* was cut to pieces, her masts and yards torn and her hull badly injured. The captain received a ball in his head and died just after Paul Jones's men had boarded the ship. His lieutenant survived him only two days. The company of the *Ranger* escaped without serious wounding except that Paul Jones lost his lieutenant.

The consternation produced in the minds of the English was indescribable, as it was to them inexplicable. The rapid succession of Jones's exploits: the descent on Whitehaven, the landing at St. Mary's, the capture of the *Drake,* overwhelmed the public mind with terror, which exhibited itself in the usual form of extravagant reports. All along the south coast watchmen reported seeing Paul Jones and his men and his ship the *Ranger.* There was a universal bustle of defensive preparations, companies of volunteers were formed (the Home Guard of the day), old forts were repaired and new ones erected.

At this point Paul Jones had to deal with a little local difficulty. He had put Lieutenant Simpson in charge of the *Drake* which was hastily repaired and made seaworthy, but Lieutenant Simpson, once he got the command of a ship, chose to regard himself as the equal of his captain. This, of course, could not be tolerated. When the ships arrived at Brest, Paul Jones had to arrest his own lieutenant. Throughout the story of Paul Jones we are always conscious that crews were mutinously-minded and that even officers were apt to question orders. It was probably because he could control this kind of incipient sedition that Paul Jones was such an outstanding leader.

Paul Jones fought a number of other actions on a grander scale than the exploits I have described. He returned to Brest with over two hundred prisoners. His exploits were acclaimed in America and in France and a price of ten thousand pounds was put upon his head in England. At the height of his success he had money difficulties. The remittances from America were held up and jealousy in the French Navy contrived to freeze funds which should have been available in France.

However, Paul Jones overcame all the difficulties and started off with a French fleet, headed by the *Pallas* and *Vengeance,* to harry the English coast. He turned up at the most unexpected places, sailing under false flags, tricking the home ships into giving him their signal codes and creating havoc wherever he went, as far north as the Humber.

Naval battles at this time, partly because they were fought at such close range, provoked an indescribable fury. This is a description by Captain Charles Johnson of a desperate sea battle which Paul Jones won in the end, defying all the odds, a battle that made the name Paul Jones one of terror throughout England, so that man, woman and child trembled at the very sound of his name:

'The *Seraphis* now fought with the actual view of sinking the enemy and her broadsides were incessant. But for the two ships being lashed together the *Bon Homme* must have struck or sunk or both. The battery of twelve-pounders was entirely silenced and abandoned. There were only two nine-pounders on the quarter deck that were not silenced. The purser working these guns was shot through the head, Paul Jones had to fill his place in person. He fought this action as if victory was assured, although all the time a superior enemy was threatening to sink the entire invading fleet. Jones's topmen kept up so well aimed a fire that if any of the enemy ventured on deck it was at the expense of his life. The British captain, Captain Pearson, signalled asking if Jones was ready to surrender. The answer was: 'No.' In fact both vessels were on fire and the gunners had to fight the flames from reaching the magazine as they were attempting to keep up their broadside. Paul Jones surveyed his ship. The rudder was off, the timbers everywhere torn to pieces, the stern-frame and transoms almost wholly cut away, while the vessel was taking in water at an alarming rate. Still Paul Jones would not yield and then he saw a sight that evoked a cheer from his men. The mainmast of the *Seraphis* shook and he thought he discerned a decrease in the enemy fire. At half past ten the flag of England which had been nailed to the mast of the *Seraphis* was struck by Captain Pearson's own hand. It was a mighty victory and it made Paul Jones into a living legend.'

Paul Jones was made an admiral of the American fleet and was used as a forceful diplomatic naval envoy by the Americans. Thus in July 1789 we find him being received in St.

Petersburg in an imperial audience, the empress decorating him with the insignia of the Order of St. Anne. Paul Jones served the Russians for a time, but could not get on with them. It was typical, of course, for men pursuing the profession of Paul Jones to hire out their services to the highest bidder and this tradition perpetuated even in England until comparatively recent times. General Gordon, for instance, after a dispute with Cairo and London, contemplated joining the service of the King of the Belgians in the Congo, but, perhaps wisely, changed his mind.

The King of Denmark gave Paul Jones an annuity of fifteen hundred crowns to be paid at Copenhagen without 'any retention'. But Paul Jones was now a sick man. He was very ill in Paris, where he died in June 1792. He was mourned both in America and France, where the National Assembly sent an official deputation to his funeral. He was only forty-six.

It is obvious that his public character was one of exceptional determination and daring, but what sort of a man was he in private? A friend describes him as: 'Of a middle, or rather inclining to a short stature, slenderly formed, with a stern countenance and a swarthy complexion, his manner authoritative and his air determined.'

He does not seem to have married, having instead a mistress only when he had time for such attachments. Some twenty years after his death a large bundle of letters was discovered in a baker's shop in New York. They turned out to be the correspondence of Paul Jones. When he left America for the last time he committed to the care of his friend, a Mr. Ross of Philadelphia, several large packages of manuscripts, letters and journals. These papers form the foundation of much that has been written concerning Paul Jones.

How can we sum up the character and the career of this unique man? He was one of the last Scotsmen to take advantage of the turbulence of his time. He was a child of the chaos of the war between America and England. He exploited confusion. He broke all the rules and yet he had some chivalry and some compassion. He was both a traitor and a hero. Constantly he made his own opportunities and was the artificer of his own success. He hardly ever obeyed any orders. He gave the orders.

Perhaps his epitaph might be: 'He did it his way.'

The American Pattern

THE height of intimidation on a grand scale in the United States came in the 'twenties and the 'thirties in the prohibition era. The outlawing of drink was resented by a large minority of the population which became a majority when the public saw the impossibility of enforcing the new laws, and the wave upon wave of gangster terror to which it gave rise.

When a law loses the support of a majority of the public, people always start to support those who break that law. Ordinary citizens who drank moderately made no bones about being supplied with whisky and gin by their bootlegger much in the same way as their grocer supplied them with sugar, salt and tea. The 14th Amendment had lost that popular support on which all laws depend for their effectiveness.

So the American gangster and bootlegger of the 'twenties and 'thirties came into the picture. He was not of necessity a hated figure. The lines of judgment were blurred by the fact that the bootleggers provided what most of the public regarded as a service to which, as free citizens exercising the right of choice, they were entitled.

Because of this the emergence of a ferocious and evil bunch of men as bosses of the bootleg racket at first passed almost unnoticed. Johnny Torrio, Al Capone and Bugs Moran were known to be gangsters controlling illicit traffic in their area of the United States. It was known that they had amassed great fortunes. It was accepted that their manors were clearly defined and that an intrusion into their territory by another gangster, who, with his own mob, was trying to muscle in on a rival's land, would lead to trouble, possibly to murder.

By a long and constant process of intimidation the public were induced to accept the theory that gangsters' business was special and apart, and not subject in any way to the control and sanctions of either the Federal or the States legislatures. It went further than this. The police, or sections of the police force, were seduced by bootleg money into ignoring bootleg business. And even the elected representatives of the people had among them a small but powerful section who had secret alliances with gangsterdom.

So men like Al Capone at the height of his dreadful power had achieved their ambition. They were a recognised part of the American establishment. They might have a bar sinister on their escutcheon but the public treated them with an awed deference.

The gangsters had created a state within a state and that is the constant and ultimate danger that democracy can never accept. Such a privileged position can never be accorded to any body of citizens, whether they be gangsters or undergraduates, or clergy or trade unions or any other section of society subject to the law.

The gangsters travelled like kings with an entourage of retainers, advisers, lawyers and strong-arm muscle men. I saw Al Capone drive up to an hotel in New York. Four cars were in the cavalcade. My driver said: 'It's Capone.'

The first car drew up just beyond the entrance while six men got out. They ranged themselves three on either side of the entrance. They were all armed. One could see the bulge of their automatics only too clearly. The second car drew up and stopped. The third man out of this was Al Capone. He walked very quickly between his guards up the steps into the foyer, a little rat of a man who yet achieved an air of complete and terrifying authority, his eyes hidden beneath dark glasses, a grey sombrero shading his face. Smartly dressed and unmistakable. I was reminded immediately of the old description of Louis XIV, whose quick walk, looking neither to the left nor right—but missing nothing—was compared to the progress of an electric hare.

The men in the second car were joined by the men in the third and fourth cars. They all swarmed in after their leader. He had arrived. There was nothing craven or hunted about Al Capone. He moved around as if he owned the place. The deference of head waiters, porters, cloakroom attendants, even managers, was accepted as his due. His king-size tips ensured that there would be no falling off in the fawning adulation.

The gangsters' women completed the picture. When rarely they appeared they shone with diamonds. There was nothing cheap or tawdry about these men. They had done what all young Americans had been taught was the aim of living and work—they had amassed great fortunes. The fact that they were murderers was all too easily overlooked. The comment was: 'These guys only kill one another. It's better to let them iron out their own disputes. That's the way it is.'

Yes, that's the way it was. But a heavy price was paid for allowing this long reign of outlaw rule, the creation of the state within the state.

The old regime of gangsters gradually died. Some were murdered, some imprisoned, or, in a few cases, achieved old age and retirement. But America had allowed the gangsters to rule by intimidation and murder for over a decade. It left a bitter scar on the American way of life. This great people had not smashed the gangs. The gangs, organised for boot-legging, had their revenue taken from them by the repeal of the 14th Amendment.

It was inevitable that the gangs, changing hands now, should look for other sources of revenue, and they found these in the increasing gambling fever, in prostitution (an old favourite), and in narcotics.

The second world war tended to halt the gangsters, partly because the authorities assumed special powers to enforce the public peace and in this they were backed by the public. Overt gangsterism on a large scale was 'unfashionable' for the duration. But it came thundering back in 1946. And the ranks of the gangsters were reinforced and strengthened by many men who, in the forces, had been taught to kill. A new and ominous situation arose.

As time went on into the 'fifties, the public began to hear of new names. They heard of one survivor of the bootleg era, an American citizen, who was said to have amassed an immense fortune estimated at a hundred million dollars. He was interested in, among other projects, gambling. Two friends of his turned up in London. The F.B.I. informed Scotland Yard of the arrival of these two characters. In fact the British police already knew of their arrival, their history, and their address in London. One was listed as one of the directors of organised crime in the United States. The other was said to control a casino in Las Vegas and to be a confidant of the former bootlegger who had achieved control of gambling in most of the Southern States of America, was the unspoken boss of Las Vegas, and was doing very nicely in Cuba until the dictator Batista fell.

In the 'fifties American crime was still mainly confined to the American continent. But in the 'sixties there were ominous signs that the crime syndicates were casting envious eyes at Britain. Why? Why should a small island of fifty-five million people attract these men who had a common market of two hundred and fifty million citizens?

There was a two-fold answer. Firstly the F.B.I., under tough and experienced leadership, was making life difficult for enterprising gentlemen in the United States. And Britain, though small as compared to the States numerically, had an interesting feature. The Britishers spent three times as much on gambling per head of the population as did American citizens. So, in fact, this great river of gold, unleashed by Lord Butler's ill-considered and ill-advised Betting Act, presented a most attractive lure to the men across the Atlantic. In addition, the Americans thought that Scotland Yard might be easier to deal with than the F.B.I. Perhaps they were misled by the courtesy and urbanity of the British police. They could not have been more mistaken.

When it became obvious that large parties of American gamblers were arriving on what purported to be gambling sprees in London, but in fact were forays designed to assess the possibilities in Britain and make the necessary contacts, the Home Secretary acted swiftly. More than twenty visitors were deported back to the United States, and these included a number of well-known figures such as Mr. George Raft, the film actor, who had never been a gangster but had become a director of the Colony Sporting Club in Berkeley Square. Meanwhile the British gangsters had not been idle. Seeing the overt threat of American competition and expertise, they closed their ranks to attempt to seize control of the gambling prize themselves. In order to do this it was necessary to enforce discipline and in order to make this plain to all those whom it might concern they were prepared to make one or two examples.

They used methods that instantly warned the police that these murders were gang executions and not domestic killings. The bomb triggered off by the self-starter of a car was a favoured device, but on more than one occasion the victim was merely shot by an assailant who vanished.

For instance, when Gomer Charles, who lived over his betting shop at Park Place, Cardiff, answered his doorbell one wet and windy December night a tall, lean man in an overcoat shot him twice through the heart and once through the eyes—and vanished. It was an execution. And it was a warning.

For the first time in Britain we were being conditioned into accepting as ordinary news items the cold-blooded execution of someone who had broken the rules. Gomer Charles was an interesting character. He had been concerned in a notorious racehorse switch some years before his death when a substituted animal won, very easily, the two o'clock race at Bath. From that time on he had had enemies, but he had nevertheless played his hand as a lone wolf, refusing to co-operate with the fraternity who were taking such matters in hand.

Race-course betting was but a part of the gambling wealth, and not the most important part. The betting shops and the large fashionable gambling casinos were much more interesting and rewarding. These were the establishments that the Americans were after and that the British gangs moved in on. It is not difficult to see what is going on. Go any day and keep a long watch on a betting shop—and see what happens. . . .

So American crime and gangsterdom with new techniques

and new know-how was having its impact on British crime. The Americans had adopted some very effective drugs and acids for immobilising those who got in their way, and these were soon to be used in the highly organised hold-ups on banks and security vans.

The whole pattern of British crime was changing. The old relationship between the police and the criminal classes was fast disappearing. This relationship had well-recognised rules. The criminals (in the days of capital punishment) did not carry arms, nor did the police. The villains did not grass and the police did not use illegal methods to make them do so. The informers were loathed by the villains but used by the police, who despised them. Most habitual criminals were well known to the police, who were familiar with their specialised skills. Because of this intimate relationship the police were often able to name, for instance, a safe-breaker before they had consulted their files.

But it was the social background of the criminal that was to alter most radically. For over a century the criminal had been a hunted, craven member of the community, a shabby outcast recognised and looked down upon as such. In the 'sixties all this was to change. The police found themselves confronted by prosperous-looking gentlemen who looked like business men and ran their criminal activities as if they were legitimate business enterprises. Many of these men had no records. They had money, organisation, a façade of respectability. They posed a new menace and a new danger to the forces of law and order.

If the American pattern of well-organised ferocity is having an increasingly menacing effect on the mode of crime in Britain it is because the two countries, in spite of great divergencies, tend to follow a somewhat similar development.

Crime feeds on money, so to follow and understand the crime pattern at any particular moment one has to ask oneself: Where is the money going?

In Britain the answer is clear. It is going into gambling. No one knows how much the total bill is, but it is between a thousand and two thousand million pounds. Gambling in the United States has increased, but much less quickly. The

British gambling explosion is without its counterpart in the States, a healthy sign for that country.

Prostitution is very much the poor relation these days, but it thrives still in the United States, while in Britain, though it still lingers on, it is a dying industry. The average young man in Britain does not have to pay money to sleep with a girl. Which leaves the practising prostitutes with a clientele of elderly men and perverts—and a greatly reduced revenue.

The third money-earner is narcotics and for three decades the United States was almost alone in making the supply of narcotics a lucrative pursuit for the gangs with money to invest. Now Britain is catching up. But still there are about half a million addicts or near-addicts in the States and probably under twenty thousand in Britain.

So the great market is America, with Britain a small but promising outlet for the future. Narcotics have been given a terrific lift by the new permissiveness. We are being asked to believe that hashish is no more harmful than whisky or tobacco—both highly addictive. It is true that hashish does not have the addictive properties of the hard drugs, heroin and cocaine. But it is the psychological preparation for conversion to these deadly drugs. Very few teenagers, either in the States or in Britain, start their drug life on the intravenous injection of heroin or the eating or drinking of morphia. They start with 'pot.' And they may remain with it until the awful time comes for them to put away childish things and graduate to the drug which will kill them.

It has been calculated that even the most restrained heroin addict does not enjoy his drug for more than eight weeks. In the early part of that time he—or she—feels that at last heaven has arrived. They can still carry on with their work, but always at the back of their minds is the evening of bliss. After this short honeymoon the marriage of the drug and the victim takes on a nightmarish quality and from then on it is purgatory, but the victim, knowing that death is ahead, almost looks forward to the day and will not willingly, on any account or for any inducement, change his manner of living—or of dying.

I

The question arises: Do those whose job it is to contain or abolish drug-taking in fact help the narcotics gangsters and their pedlars? The American and British methods of dealing with the matter are quite different. American law says that drug addiction is a crime and a drug addict a criminal. British law only says that the illicit possession of certain drugs constitutes a crime. Possession alone is not a crime. It must be unlawful possession. Why is this? The answer is that the doctors in Britain are empowered to prescribe drugs to confirmed addicts in 'moderate' quantities. In London one can see them crowding around the authorised chemist to obtain their stuff perfectly legally. Moreover, much of the addictive trade is done on the national health, which means that you and I pay for it. It seems a very strange situation.

However, in spite of this, until five years ago British methods could claim success where American methods had clearly failed. They can no longer make this claim with any credibility or conviction. Hashish has become fashionable among the young and this unfortunately includes the very young. In certain areas and cities the growth of the drug habit is spreading at an alarming rate. Is containment, in fact, possible? Do not such addicts welcome it as securing their supply which they can supplement from other sources?

This poses the question: Would not arrest and imprisonment without treatment be in the best interests of the addicts? Some would die, but would not those who survived be cured? The communists in China outlawed opium by hanging a few of the addicts. In the West we cannot do this, but it may well be that the sternest methods are the most effective and so, in the long run, the kindest, inflicting less horror.

The profit to be made out of narcotics is completely concealed. We only know it must be immense. Half a pound of opium can be bought very cheaply in the countryside of Laos. The same amount, especially if refined into morphine, will fetch a small fortune in Britain or in America.

For years I was much concerned as a lawyer in cases that entailed the trade in narcotics. Much of it came to Europe by way of Beirut or Cairo. But perhaps a larger amount reached the United States—a larger market than the rest of the world combined—by sea and air. The ports of despatch were Rangoon, Bangkok and Hong Kong. Unfortunately for America, the Vietnam war has given many thousands of U.S. soldiers a taste for 'pot'. These men smoke it every day to relieve the boredom of inaction, to steady their nerves if they are hunting Vietcong, or for sexual stimulation in the brothels of Saigon. Perhaps a Western nation has never before been corrupted on this scale. These men will take the habit with them when they return and a new injection of ardent addicts will be on the role of those who pay the tribute that the illegal suppliers demand in the black market. It is a grim relic of war, a bitter and enduring memento of a long and tragic affair.

One cannot study the crime pattern in America nor its repercussions in Britain without asking oneself: Are the news media, television in particular, partly responsible for the glamorising of the gangsters and even for the startling increase in the bread and butter of crime, the hold-ups, gambling and narcotics.

Certainly British television has cashed in mercilessly on the dramatic side of crime. The crime series is always a potential winner in the rating stakes and in these crime epics killing is taken for granted. The pistol is pointed. The gun is fired. The victim collapses and dies. It seems to be taken for granted that that is what happens in real life. Likewise do the drug documentaries really help? Many, perhaps most, drug addicts start experimenting, confident that they can break away at will. Within a very few weeks they realise they are prisoners of a vile mistress.

Television revels in the violent hold-up because it is a story natural. The bank with its pompous manager and his assistants. The atmosphere of calm respectability as if nothing illegal can ever happen here. While all the time we know that the gang, like a rodent ulcer, are working their way through the defences. It is high drama, but the networks employ specialists on these films and quite often they pursue the intricacies of the story with such fervour and ingenuity that they suggest new methods even to the most accomplished robbers . . .

Television can give us great entertainment and through its documentaries bring the world to our screen. Its news we could not now do without, but we might pause to ask ourselves if murder, burglary and narcotics are not, in fact, nursed and nourished by the television screen. If the crime wave recedes nothing will be done to stop this, but if, as seems possible, the wave becomes a tidal wave of monstrous proportions, if again, in America, a state within a state is created and if that pattern is reproduced in Britain, then we shall have to impose limits of violence and crime on the television screen.

The most damaging lesson that British criminals have learnt from the American world of crime is that violence pays and that terror is the best instrument of crime. Get the public cowed. Then they won't give any trouble. Persuade the young that the police are pigs. Then no one will help the police. Make a hero of the gangster and a heroine of his woman. After all, they are anti-pig. What more do you want?

I have not mentioned one most important aspect of modern crime and intimidation both in the States and in this country. The protection racket. The public know that if once they pay protection money they are in the power of a gang. Yet they pay. Little restaurants in New York pay, and eating places in Soho pay. Many betting shops pay and big casinos pay.

Why? It is not only fear. All these businesses can make money easily if they are left in peace. If there is any kind of disturbance or incident they suffer immediately and tragically. So the payment of a comparatively small weekly sum seems only sensible insurance. But, of course, it is not. The rates can be raised at any time at the whim of the extortionists. Danegeld never did get rid of the Dane. Peace is purchased for a time and at a price. . . .

The protection racket, which has reached gigantic proportions in the United States, is the most difficult crime for the police to kill. Those who are protected will not speak. They are afraid of being branded as informers, of breaking the unspoken agreement with the racketeers. 'No one says anything.' Payments in cash are never receipted. No money can be proved to have passed. Moreover, the police tend to be inundated with what seem to be more serious crimes—murder, arson, theft, embezzlement, riot and the ever-present hold-up. So the patient investigation needed to break a protection racket, the impersonations, the watching, the long and tedious interviews are never made. The racket goes on—smoothly.

Intimidation by the criminals of the public can only come about as it has done recently if the criminals feel themselves on top. In Britain the number of attacks on the public by gangsters, inflicted while carrying out a raid, has increased a hundred-fold. Very often the shot in the stomach or the broken leg seem to be deliberately inflicted as a warning on the principle: Maybe it was not necessary but it will scare them another time.

So the members of the public prepared to 'have a go' and attempt to stop or even to arrest fleeing bandits is very small. The bonds that should bind the public to the police have been weakened. Who wants to undergo the agony and inconvenience of being shot? The expensive treatment. The time lost from work. The stay in hospital. Perhaps never achieving complete recovery. After all, most property-holders are insured. Why sacrifice oneself for the insurance companies? So the public decides to be smart and leave evil alone.

The lesson seems to be that in crime intimidation pays. And it pays rich and continuing dividends. Because of this the black banner of the gangsters is riding high in Britain, America and in most countries in the Western world.

Who is going to win the battle in the 'seventies? Will the gangsters win and rule again as wealthy magnates who are tolerated and feared? Or will there be a revival of public spirit, uniting all the forces of law and order and the general public to smash the menace that has now become so blatant and seems to jeer at our efforts to keep it at bay.

No one knows the answer. But, having spent my life among criminals or in the study of crime, I would not like to bet on it.

12

The Firm

THE long catalogue of English crime commonly pursues a steady pattern. Yet sometimes it takes on a character so bizarre and so terrifying that one realises that anything can happen in Britain at any time. In the Victorian age, for twenty years, the London underworld was dominated by a seemingly respectable barrister-at-law who followed his profession in the courts by day and pursued his complicated and lucrative criminal activities by night. This was against the pattern, an outrage of cunning, duplicity and exploitation of the perfect cover.

The advent of the Kray brothers is another such defiance of all the rules that are said to govern crime in Britain, whether in London or the provinces. For the three Krays, Charles the eldest and the twins, Reginald and Ronald, imposed a Mafia-type of rule and extortion on clubs by the terror they inspired. They would have been perfectly in place in the America of the prohibition era, but they operated in the London of the 'sixties. The English police, of course, have never carried arms, and the Krays were trained fighters, having graduated in the boxing ring. Their natural ferocity was their stock-in-trade. A newspaper reporter who often drank with them told me: 'The twins, Ronald and Reginald, could create an atmosphere of terror whenever they wanted it. They did not have to say a word. Their manner was so forbidding, their whole aspect, when they had been crossed, was so menacing that any club they entered was on tenterhooks. In the East End they were not charged for drinks. Usually the proprietor was called to propitiate them. But when he came they baited him with indescribable cruelty and cunning. The entry of the Krays and their henchmen was like an old Bogart film when the gangsters appeared on the scene. One just could not believe it was happening, but it was happening, and before one's eyes.'

Who were they, the Krays? How came it that they became rich men who murdered to preserve their authority? How did they manage to contact the American Mafia? How did they collect a circle of 'friends' in show business and in fashion? The story begins in Shoreditch, which is the inner hardcore stamping ground of the London Cockney with a population now as varied as a Chinese menu. English, Poles, Jews, Jamaicans, Negroes, Indians, now swarm together through the East End of London. Shoreditch is tough, poor, drab, and each man has to fend for himself.

In the 1930s Shoreditch was a vast slum. This was the era of the great depression and the hunger marches, and it was into that era that the Krays were born.

As the elder brother, Charles, is always the figure in the background, never actually involved when violence and death flared, so we concentrate on the twins, Ronald and Reginald. They were born to Mrs. Violet Kray, whose husband was a furniture dealer, at 68 Steen Street, Shoreditch, on 24th October 1933. They were unusually strong for twins, and very close to one another, so that, from an early age, they always acted in unison. This trait never left them and it had a bearing on the crime empire they created. Between them there was an extrasensory perception. The one would know at once the thoughts of the other, and if they were parted each would know if the other had encountered difficulty or danger. Moreover, neither twin would allow the other to break away and forge any independent links. At school in Daniel Street, Shoreditch, if one fought they both fought. You could not attack Reginald without Ronald. They became tough but by no means tearaways. Their fitness was partly due to the tuition of their grandfather, an old-time pugilist, 'Cannonball' Lee, still alive, who taught them how to use their fists and keep fit. They responded so well to their mentor that their first inclination was to make boxing their career. This they did for a time as young men in their early twenties. They had their share of success, but the money in boxing, except at the very top of the heavyweight class, was poor and the twins had no intention of ending up as the victims of punch-drunk poverty.

Usually in tracing criminal careers the symptoms of the disease that is to develop are discernible very early. Ian Brady, the Moors murderer, was a fascinating if repulsive example of this. He was a torturer, revelling in the infliction of pain from his early schooldays. Not so the Krays. As children they appeared to be exemplary. I say 'appeared to be', for the Krays were always anxious, right up to the end, to make a good impression. But those who came into contact with them as boys detected nothing sinister. They thought that they were a fine, upstanding pair, polite and charming.

When they were evacuated during the bombing of London to a doctor's family near Ipswich the family verdict on them was: 'The Kray boys were very nice. They never gave any trouble. We were sorry when they left.'

The Krays continued to collect these little quiet accolades until they were young men, and apparently they cherished them, for even when they had quit professional boxing and taken up the exploitation and extortion of London clubs as their business, even when they had made their Firm a household word for terror and were accompanied everywhere by an entourage of faithful thugs who did their bidding, they tried desperately hard to keep their previous reputations. At the height of their career, after they had been acquitted on extortion charges arising out of a newspaper dispute, they offered a retainer to a public-relations firm to improve their image. The firm in question made enquiries and declined the commission.

Yet, without any expert aid, the Krays did quite well in putting over a picture of benevolence and generosity. They got themselves photographed with Lord Boothby and entertained celebrities such as Judy Garland and Sophie Tucker. They bought a country house, the Brooks, at Bidelston in Surrey, and the villagers thought them wonderful. There was nothing the busy London gentlemen would not do to help along local charity and they never forgot a birthday or a promise. It seemed to those who knew them only as the celebrities they had now become that it was their natural kindness that distinguished the Krays from their humdrum fellow citizens.

The clubs that they operated directly show the trend of their thinking. They started with the Double R in Bow Road. This was an East End club. It did not satisfy them for long, so the Kentucky Club took its place. This was lush and well decorated. Their stage friends gave them ideas on modern décor. But even the Kentucky, with its American overtones, was not enough. They wanted to attract the big names—and the generous spenders. So they launched Esmeralda's Barn in Knightsbridge. They were moving west, into society, into the golden mile, into the heart of the West End, into the London that until now had been for them a strange and almost forbidden country. For these brothers were children of the East End. They always loved it and even when in the end the law caught up with them their real home was their parents' house in Vallance Road. Spiritually they were still children of Shoreditch. For them Esmeralda's Barn was both a challenge and an adventure.

It was their club business that led them into the extortion racket. London clubs are apt to take money very easily. England is still the second or third richest country in the world and the West End of London by far the most concentrated area of inherited and earned wealth anywhere. For discreet luxury it has no peer. It was here that the Krays now operated.

Their extortion business followed the classical pattern. 'Pay up or be molested.' They paid up. The Krays had become kings of all the seedier London clubs. The few very select gambling clubs spent a fortune in keeping the Krays and their agents out of their premises. To do this they had to hire their own very private little armies.

The Krays hit the peak of their public renown when David Bailey, an eminently respectable society photographer, included them in a lush, illustrated book of celebrities that cost three guineas and sold extremely well. Lord Snowdon, Princess Margaret's husband, was included in the collection, and for the Krays to be in this company, even if only by proxy, was a major achievement for them. They revelled in it. This showed that they had really arrived.

The twins were not all gore and glory. They had their tragedies. Reginald Kray's marriage broke up and not long after his wife Frankie committed suicide. He was desolate. The Krays had an un-English streak of deep sentimentality and fervid family devotion. Reginald was moved by Frankie's death to write this awful, but none the less deeply felt, epitaph:

IF

If I could climb upon a passing cloud
That would drift your way
I would not ask for a more beautiful day.
Perhaps I would pass a rainbow,
With nature's colours so beautifully aglow,
If you were there at the Journey's End
I would know
It was the beginning and not the end.

When they were carousing with their drinking companions —they never drank too much—the twins would sing their Cockney songs, rendering them with immense pathos, so that tears streamed down their cheeks. It was not put on. It was natural to them. But business was business and when the Firm was meeting under the chairmanship of Ronald, respectfully referred to as 'the colonel', sentiment took a very back seat. The money was forthcoming or those who were withholding it should know their displeasure which took explosive forms. To be the victims of a Kray terror attack was not a pleasant experience.

In the end the Krays became internationally minded. Their extraordinary fraud on the Bank of Nova Scotia shows their organisation developing. One of the factors that induced Scotland Yard to strike when it did was the Kray interest in the Mafia and the visit to England of a Mafia agent who had come to enquire if the Firm would enter into a transatlantic partnership.

In another year the Krays would have formed links and had contacts as powerful as any in international crime. They were only smashed just in time. And they were smashed only as the result of the most secret and massive police operation of all time.

To the end they could not believe that their golden life was ending. It would go on for ever. They were above the law now. They were too strong to be caught and held and tried and convicted. But this was an illusion. Without their knowing it, their closest henchmen had ratted on them. The East End was very tired of them. The once-intimidated public was prepared to talk once the Krays were inside. So they were arrested at dawn and in bed.

At the end of their long trial, during which they showed unheard-of contempt and defiance, at last they heard the words that they had always believed could never be spoken.

Mr. Justice Melford Stevenson addressing Ronald Kray said: 'I am not going to waste words on you. I sentence you to life imprisonment and, because I think society has earned a rest from your activities, I recommend that you be detained for thirty years.'

To Reginald the judge addressed an even briefer sentence for a similar period. It was the end. But the Krays were still very much in the news, for the sentence went against all the trends of modern penal psychiatry and the new penology. The debate is still raging.

The three brothers from Shoreditch rose to dominate the extortion business of the London underworld, murdered for business and were on the verge of creating an international syndicate of crime when at last the law caught up with them.

May we never see their like again.

When any of their associates crossed them seriously, or betrayed them, the Krays resorted to murder. Let us look at two of their murders, that of Jack the Hat McVitie, and the murder at the Blind Beggar public house.

I was present at the magistrates' court proceedings as well as at the trial at the Old Bailey, and the following is a record of my notes taken at this time.

First Jack the Hat.

The public, quick to forget, had not thought about the Krays during the late summer and early autumn. We did not expect to have to return to Bow Street,* but here we were again listening to a charge of murder which in its savagery and bestiality surpassed anything to which we had previously listened.

Briefly the prosecution alleged that Ronald Kray had held a character named Jack the Hat McVitie, while Reginald Kray stabbed him to death in a flat in Evering Road, Stoke Newington. As usual Charles Kray is the sinister but dominating figure hovering in the background and we are not surprised to hear that he and others are charged with hindering the arrest of the murderers.

I listened carefully as the actual charges were read out to the Krays, who were back in the dock taking up the exact positions they had previously assumed. I thought they looked older. Charles, the elder brother, still maintained his air of inscrutable authority, but the twins, Ronald and Reginald, seemed much less composed. They fidgeted with their handkerchiefs and conversed together whenever they could in muttered whispers. They gave the impression of being violently resentful of something and before long we were to know the reason for this.

The clerk of the court read the charges.

Ronald and Reginald Kray, together with Christopher Lambrianou, Anthony Lambrianou, Ronald Albert Bender, and Anthony Thomas Barry, were accused of murdering McVitie in a flat in East Hackney on 16 October, 1967. I noticed that the youngest of the gang was twenty-six and the oldest, the twins themselves, thirty-four. Only Charles Kray, at forty-one, was in a slightly different age category. He was charged with Frederick Gerald Foreman, Cornelious John Whitehead and Albert Joseph Donaghue with hindering the arrest of the murderers and being an accessory after the fact.

The whole story as it was unfolded in court was a terrible one.

For some reason which was never revealed at the trial,

---

* The previous case had concerned the 'Mad Axeman'.

the Kray brothers had sentenced Jack the Hat McVitie to death. What McVitie had done to incur the wrath of the Krays perhaps we shall never know, but the pattern of the previous charges shows that the Krays ran the underworld of the East End on the explicit understanding that they were absolute rulers. To deny them anything or to frustrate their designs in any way was a capital offence and, of course, to cross their path deliberately or to inform against them was the most serious crime of all, and it was the deliberate policy of the Krays that no one in the East End should ever be allowed to endanger their position in this way without immediate and terrible retribution.

The prosecution called a number of witnesses, but the one who impressed me most was the young man, perhaps twenty-five years of age, fair and fairly well spoken. He was smartly dressed and appeared to answer the questions put to him without hesitation. He described a night at the end of October 1967, when he and his brother, the two Lambrianous and McVitie left the Regency Club about 1.30 a.m. to go to a party. The Lambrianou brothers and McVitie walked ahead. He and his brother followed downstairs to a basement room. There was a short scuffle with McVitie and then Reginald Kray produced a knife. The young man went on:

'McVitie tried to jump out of the window, but Ronnie Kray and Bender pulled him back. Reggie Kray stabbed him two or three times in the stomach, twisting the knife. Bender and Ronnie Kray were both holding McVitie. McVitie then fell on the floor. Ronnie Kray said: "Kill him, Reg." It looked as if Reggie Kray was going to stab him in the neck. My brother and I ran out of the room.

'Sometime after that I saw Anthony Lambrianou in the Regency Club. I asked him what had happened to McVitie. Anthony Lambrianou said: "Just forget all about it. Don't say nothing about it".'

Jack the Hat was never seen again.

Some of the most damning evidence on this and the following day was given by Ronald Joseph Hart, who described how he disposed of a gun and a knife after the murder of

Jack the Hat McVitie. For some reason the Kray brothers took the greatest exception to the evidence of Joseph Hart and they began to shout out remarks against him and were constantly silenced by the magistrate, who ordered the remarks to be inserted in the record and warned the accused that conduct of this kind could only damage their own interests. Basically, of course, these prosecution witnesses were all subject to the grievous handicap that they had in some way been implicated in the matter. For instance, Joseph Hart said that he had been present during the stabbing.

When Joseph Hart said that he had heard Foreman, one of the accused, tell Charles Kray that when the body of McVitie was taken from a car 'it had a horrible film over it' Foreman shouted out: 'You're a liar, that never happened.'

Mr. Geraint Reece, the magistrate, ordered Foreman's remark to be recorded on the deposition, but Ronald Kray then called out to Hart: 'You liar.' Foreman then said again: 'He is a liar.' Reginald Kray stood up in the dock and said: 'I call him a liar.' Another defendant made the significant remark: 'He is a rat as well.' All these remarks were recorded on the deposition. Joseph Hart continued to give his evidence, but Ronald Kray again shouted: 'He is known as a liar all over the East End.'

The magistrate was now getting impatient with the defendants and he said: 'I warn Ronald Kray not to shout threatening remarks to the witness.'

But Christopher Lambrianou then stood up and said: 'The Bible says though shalt not bear false witness against thy neighbour. That is what he is doing.'

This was the most unruly scene that I had witnessed in an English court during the many years I have attended criminal trials in one capacity or another. The magistrate decided that it would be advisable to have a short recess and, addressing counsel, he said: 'Would you talk to your clients and tell them that shouting from the dock is prejudicial and does not help them at all?'

The Bar bowed, indicating that they would do this. However, as the defendants left the court one of them—I could not tell which it was—shouted out to Joseph Hart: 'Why don't you tell the truth just for a change?'

Again Joseph Hart continued his evidence. He said that he drove to the flat of a man named Harry Hopwood where he washed a knife and gun because Ronnie Kray had told him to do so. He and Hopwood then drove to Ronnie Kray's Aunt May in the Vallance Road. There they picked up some clothing. On the way back to Hopwood's flat he threw the gun and knife into the canal at Queensbridge Road. When a black automatic gun was handed up to the witness by Mr. Kenneth Jones, Q.C., Hart said: 'I don't actually recognise this one, but it is the same size.'

Joseph Hart said that when he returned to the Hopwood flat Ronald and Reginald Kray were having a bath. 'I washed the hair of Reggie Kray. He was not able to do it himself because he had cut his hand.'

Hart went on: 'The twins left their clothing in a pile on the floor. I put all three suits of clothing in a case, which was to be taken away and burnt by a man named Percy.' Ronnie Kray then told Hopwood to burn the one pound and ten shilling notes that had been in their pockets. Joseph Hart saw Hopwood burn the money and the ashes were washed down the sink.

Joseph Hart said that Ronnie Bender came to the flat and said he had got rid of the body 'over the water'. Hart thought that this meant on the other side of the Thames—on the South Bank.

Charles Kray arrived at the flat and Ronnie Kray said, pointing at his brother, 'He has just done McVitie.'

At the end of the evidence of Joseph Hart Counsel asked him if he knew why Reginald Kray should wish to murder Jack McVitie. Joseph Hart's answer was not a satisfactory one. He said he had heard the Kray twins in dispute on many occasions and on one occasion had heard Ronnie say to Reggie: 'I have done my one, it is time you done your one.' This was just before McVitie was killed.

Mr. Ivan Lawrence, representing Ronald Kray, then cross-examined Joseph Hart.

Hart was also cross-examined by Mr. Colin Cunningham,

representing Anthony Lambrianou. Joseph Hart admitted being a member of the Kray Firm. When he was cross-examined by Mr. Ronald Gray for Foreman, Hart said there were about twelve members of the Firm. He said he did not know whether the members of the Firm did anything else, but the Krays 'looked after them'.

The following day we were confronted by the inevitable blonde wrapped in a fairly luxurious fur coat. She was a Mrs. Skinner, but was known in Kray circles as Blonde Carol. Blonde Carol lived in the Stoke Newington flat where Jack the Hat McVitie was said to have been stabbed to death. She gave her evidence in a penetrating whisper, but one had the impression that this was not her habitual tone of voice. I could not determine her age. She was over twenty-five and less than forty-five, possibly about thirty-three. She was carefully made-up and seemed completely composed. She never looked once at the Krays in the dock but repeated her evidence as if it was a lesson she had learned by heart. This is what she said:

'I was in waiting for people to arrive when there was a knock on the door. I answered it, and it was Ronald and Reginald Kray and a few of their friends.

'They asked me if I was expecting them and I said I wasn't, but that I was having a party and was waiting for other people.

'They came in and went downstairs into the basement living room.

'I went across the road and asked a friend of mine if I could take my party into her flat. When some of my friends arrived I sent them across the road. I stayed for some time in the basement room with the Krays and their friends.

'Besides the Kray twins the people there were Ronald Bender (one of the men accused of murder), a man named Hart, his girl friend Vickie, and Reggie Kray's girl friend, Carol.

'Later, when I was talking to Vickie, Ronnie Kray called her over and said something to her. I heard her say: "What shall I tell her?"

'Then she said something to me and we went over the road

to the other party. The other Carol stayed but came over about fifteen minutes later.

'I left this party at about four o'clock and went back to my own flat. We were just going downstairs when Bender came up wearing a pair of my little boy's socks over his hands.

'He said: "Where are you going?" I said: "We are going downstairs." He said: "You can't go down there at the moment."

'When I asked him why, he said: "There's been a little bit of trouble down there and we are just tidying up the mess."

'I answered him: "I live here."

'Then Bender asked me to wait in another room for a little, so I went into a bedroom.

'Bender looked worried and frightened as he talked to me.

'Christopher Lambrianou was also in the flat. I saw him carrying a plastic bowl. He was also wearing socks over his hands.

'From where I stood it looked like blood in the bowl. I think it was water and blood. He took the bowl to the toilet.

'I noticed that the bedspread had gone and Bender told me the carpet would also have to go, but I was not to worry, it would be replaced.'

Blonde Carol went on to say that a Connie Whitehead and Vickie came into the flat and Connie said the whole place would have to be scrubbed. They scrubbed everything, including the floors and the walls, the doors, the handles, the light switches, some records and a record player. After they had left Blonde Carol and George Plummer, with whom she was living, folded up the carpet and saw drops of blood around the edges. She insisted that no one told her what had happened.

However, when she woke up next morning she found Bender in the flat. He came into the bedroom and asked to take away the top blanket. She found that the carpet and underfelt had already gone from the living room.

Bender said to the witness: 'You had better go away for a while.' She asked him where she was to go and he said, 'Jersey.' Blonde Carol said that would not really be possible.

K

Finally Blonde Carol said she was given forty pounds at the Regency Club to buy a new carpet and some other replacements for the flat. Later when Vickie was with her she saw a fine spray of red marks which seemed to be blood on the walls of the flat. After this Albert Donaghue came to re-decorate the room. It was completely re-decorated, Blonde Carol admitted that later she was paid another thirty or forty pounds.

Some weeks later Blonde Carol consulted a solicitor after she had had a visit from Scotch Ian.

The evidence of Joseph Hart and Blonde Carol was typical of most of the evidence in the series of charges brought against the Kray brothers. In every case the witness had been deeply implicated in the surrounding events of the terrible crime that was said to have been committed. Could the witnesses then be relied upon? They had the strongest possible motive for giving the kind of evidence which the police were seeking, but this did not necessarily mean that they were lying. There must have been people who were not members of the Firm but who had witnessed the killing of Jack the Hat McVitie. Blonde Carol appeared to be one of these. She had not been seriously disturbed by cross-examination. When defending counsel pointed out to her that she was deeply involved in the matter, that the murder had taken place in her flat, and that she had allowed all traces of the murder to be removed, and that further she had received considerable sums of money to restore her flat, she purred in reply: 'What could I do? I was completely in their power. I had nothing to do with the murder.'

To me this rang true. I also had the impression that the magistrate was inclined to believe Blonde Carol and it was noticeable that the defendants did not make a demonstration against her by shouting abuse as they had done in the case of Joseph Hart.

My reaction to the evidence as a whole at this stage was that a great deal of it was suspect because of the admitted motivation which was the self-preservation of the witnesses, but in spite of this a picture was building up of a completely ruthless gang dominated by the three Kray brothers who had terrorised the East End of London and built up a crime syndicate as ferocious and as efficient as any in the long catalogue of crime, and in many respects new to the English crime scene.

The murder of Jack the Hat was horrible, but that of George Cornell at the Blind Beggar public house on 1 March 1966 was more cold-blooded—more terrifying.

The English public house, usually called 'the pub' or 'the local', is a unique institution. Attempts have been made to reproduce it abroad and they have always failed. I think they failed because a pub is more than licensed drinking premises. It is a club with an unlimited membership. It is governed by unwritten rules of decorum and behaviour. Thus, though you may enter into conversation with anyone in a pub, you do not talk to a customer who obviously wants to be left alone. You do not become bitter or angry, and the general tone of the place is friendly, quiet and orderly. The beer no doubt helps the general mellifluous atmosphere. Both sexes and all ages (over eighteen) use pubs, many of which serve excellent food as well as drink. In the winter there is a fire blazing which makes the copper coaching horns and the brass harness which is hung on the walls gleam cheerfully. Pubs in the East End are really no different from those in the West End of London. It is perfectly well known that dangerous characters patronise East End pubs, but they too observe the rules when they do so.

So that at 8.30 p.m. on the night of 13th March 1966 the saloon bar of the Blind Beggar public house was pursuing the even tenor of its ways. George Cornell, a small-time criminal, was sipping a double whisky with two companions. The barmaid was joining in the conversation occasionally, but attending to other customers to keep them happy and supplied and when she had nothing better to do was polishing the glasses.

The clock which was fixed to the wall above the bar showed that the time was almost exactly half past eight when two men walked in from the street through the swing door that had the words Saloon Bar engraved on the glass. It was a cold night, almost freezing, and a gust of cold air followed them into the warm bar.

George Cornell looked round and said jovially: 'Well, look who's here.' They were the last words he ever spoke because the first man, who was Ronald Kray, drew a gun from his pocket and shot Cornell through the eyes at a range of about six feet. George Cornell slumped from his stool on to the floor. He was dying and was shortly dead. Meanwhile the second man, John Alexander Barrie, fired two shots, one into the wall and one along the bar counter. This had the not unnatural result of terrifying the other customers, who ducked into crouching positions where they saw very little of what was happening. The two bullets fired by Barrie became embedded in the furniture and were recovered. The two men, having committed their murder, then walked quietly out of the pub through the door they had entered by and vanished. It was a murder which Mr. Kenneth Jones, Q.C., rightly described in these terms: 'You may think it was horrifying effrontery, deadly effrontery, for two men to walk into a public house in this land on any evening and there, in cold blood, slay another human being.'

I think it is fair to say that the sense of outrage which this incident provoked when the murder was described in court was greater than that which would have been aroused in many other countries, because for so long Great Britain has prided itself on keeping all violence in control with an unarmed police force who are able to maintain their authority because they have the backing of the public.

As Mr. Jones continued to outline the prosecution case it became clear that he had to overcome one major difficulty. The customers in the bar had either seen nothing or had vanished soon after the murderers had left. For them the writing was on the wall. If the Kray gang could do this and get away with it, they were the most dangerous thugs in Europe. Obviously they would not hesitate for a moment to murder anyone who informed against them or anyone who dared to give evidence against them in a court of law. A blanket of silence shrouded all those who had been at the Blind Beggar public house that night. However, there was the barmaid. Now she knew the customers of the Blind Beggar. She knew Cornell. She knew Barrie and most important of all she knew Ronald Kray. She had instantly recognised the two gunmen as they came in through the door. She had seen Ronald Kray murder Cornell and she had seen Barrie fire his diversionary shots. She had been standing a few feet away when Cornell had said: 'Well, look who's here.' She had seen him slump from his stool after he had been shot and, from her position crouching behind the bar, she had seen the two gunmen leave. It was all going to depend on the barmaid. If she had the courage to give her evidence without hedging, Ronald Kray was as good as convicted, but if she was going to be broken down by cross-examination or intimidated by the Krays in the dock into prevarication or silence, then there was no saying how the case might go. She proved to be a reliable and brave witness.

I have seldom sat in a court more silent and enthralled by the opening speech of prosecuting counsel. This was the story that Mr. Kenneth Jones outlined to the jury.

After the shooting Ronald Kray and Barrie left the Blind Beggar, leaving Cornell dying on the floor. Two friends with whom he had been drinking quickly vanished, and two customers who had been in another smaller bar ducked down so that they could not see anything. The barmaid, terrified by what she had seen, fled to the cellar. The publican, who had been upstairs, came down and telephoned for an ambulance. It was eight minutes after the murder. Cornell actually died in hospital two hours later. A bullet had passed through his brain and out of the back of his skull.

That evening the Kray twins and a number of their friends, including Barrie, had been having a drink in the Lion public house, Tapp Street, which was known as Maggie's. It was from this convivial party that Ronald Kray and Barrie strolled round to commit the murder, after which they returned to Maggie's. The party immediately broke up, most of them driving off in their cars to Walthamstow. Reginald Kray and Ronald got into a car telling the driver to drive carefully. They did not want to be stopped by a police-man. Reginald said to the driver: 'Ronnie has just shot Cornell.' Ronald Kray washed his hands with great care and changed all his clothes in a public house at Walthamstow.

Obviously they were apprehensive lest some speck of blood might have impregnated the suit or perhaps even some particles of the atmosphere might have attached themselves to the clothing which could be identified as characteristic of the Blind Beggar by the police science laboratories. The twins then went to a flat nearby, but soon left there for a flat in Stoke Newington, presumably because they thought London was too hot to hold them. Neither man went anywhere near their home in Vallance Road, Stepney. They did, however, send two men to the house for changes of clothing. They also posted two men at the house in case Cornell's friends should visit the house on a mission of revenge. The Kray parents were still living there. When, in the end, Ronald and Reginald Kray were arrested they both pleaded not guilty at the police station. Barrie denied being at the Blind Beggar public house at all at the time of the murder, saying: 'I did not shoot Cornell. I wish I could tell you what happened but I'd get shot'.

Although the direct evidence of the killing was going to depend on the testimony of the barmaid, there was quite a lot of corroborative circumstantial detail. It was admitted that the whole gang were in the neighbourhood on the night of the murder. It could be proved that they had driven away to change their clothes as quickly as possible and it also could be proved that they had vanished to Stoke Newington and posted a guard on their own house in Vallance Road. This did not seem to be the conduct of men who had nothing to do with the murder.

At this point I did not know how good or how bad a witness the barmaid would be. The question which perturbed me was: How did they possibly think they could get away with it?

They did not wear any masks. No kind of disguise was resorted to. They could have shot Cornell as he left the pub in the street outside and escaped in the confusion with little risk of being identified. Why did they do it so publicly, so brazenly, as if courting a conviction? The only possible answer appeared to be that the murder was a gesture of terrifying defiance and menace. These men really believed they were above and beyond the law. They thought that no one could touch them. Wherever they went in the East End they saw that they inspired fear and instant obedience, but the East End was not the whole of London. They must have known from their previous encounters with the police that Scotland Yard were likely at some time to go all out to convict them. They were drunk with power of a particularly revolting kind. That power had corrupted them and distorted their judgment.

The psychology of terror has rules of its own.

Terror was the weapon used by the American gangsters in their heyday and it is still used extensively in the United States. It was a fairly new development in Britain. The terror consists essentially in a threat: Do what we want or you will suffer. The way in which it is intended one should suffer is not explained. This, of course, adds to the fear and the intimidation. It may be that one will be blinded by acid thrown into one's eyes. It may be that one will be forced to endure electric shock treatment on sensitive parts of the body. It may be that one will merely be subjected to obscene and terrifying threats. Or possibly one will meet the kind of end that George Cornell met.

After the magistrates' long hearing the case moved to the Old Bailey for the trial itself and the final drama.

At the start of the trial on the 28 April 1969 the presiding judge had to calm the Krays more than once. Mr. Kenneth Jones, Q.C., who again was prosecuting, seemed to incur the wrath of the brothers. Ronald Kray on, more than one occasion, shouted at him defiantly, calling him 'a big slob'.

Reginald Kray complained that Sergeant Lloyd Hughes and Superintendent Leonard Read were sneering at him.

'They keep sneering at me. If he likes to come round to the back of the dock with me, if you will let him, or come downstairs, I will deal with it.'

The judge did not think that this was a good idea and said calmly: 'Now, now, Mr. Kray, keep control of yourself. I will take care of anything like that.'

The early histrionics of the trial made the Old Bailey appear more like an American television court-room drama, but the judge soon asserted his discipline and the trial then settled down to a more conventional pattern.

The case for the Crown against the Krays for the murder of Cornell and of Jack the Hat a year later took up the first day of the trial.

The brothers, for the first time, became subdued and morose. They must have realised that a formidable case on the two murder charges had been prepared against them. That morning, when they had entered the court, they had shown a truculence and defiance of the judge, the jury and the police which I have never seen equalled in an English court.

It had been decided that in order to assist the jury in identifying individual prisoners they should wear numbered placards, but when the police moved to carry this out, Reginald Kray stormed at the judge: 'Is this a court of law or a cattle market?' This outburst electrified the other prisoners in the dock, who joined in the protest. There was an uproar such as the Old Bailey can never have seen before. The prisoners were sent down to the cells and Mr. Justice Melford Stevenson conferred with counsel in his room. It was decided that numbers should be put in front of the dock and a seating plan of the dock handed to the jury. In ordering this the judge said that he had noticed that the prisoners regarded the wearing of labels as 'inconsistent with their dignity'.

The day which had started with a minor victory for the Krays now ended on a grim note. We all realised that the first murder case at the Blind Beggar depended on the evidence of the barmaid, while the killing of McVitie could only be proved by persons heavily implicated in the crime themselves.

Nevertheless, at last, the net was closing round the men in the dock.

I was given a seat in the solicitors' row during the trial and had a perfect view of the proceedings. When I had listened to the manner in which Jack the Hat McVitie met his death I thought: Nothing can be more revolting, more terrifying than this. But, in fact, the killing of Cornell in the Blind Beggar pub was more sinister, more evil. For Cornell was openly and deliberately executed in public. His death was intended as a dreadful warning to whom it might concern. And it concerned potentially every member of the public. The Krays were saying not only 'We defy the law' but 'We are the law'.

Had they not been convicted, London would have become a city of fear. The smashing of the Firm was the most significant achievement of the Metropolitan Police Force in this century.

Three evil and savage men had, at last, been caught, convicted, and sentenced.

13

Intimidation, Yesterday

I N this book, apart from the chapter on Paul Jones, we have been dealing with twentieth-century intimidation, and we have advanced the theory that intimidation has been increasing in various fields while adopting new methods which it has not been possible so far effectively to check.

It may well be that since the turn of the century, and especially during the decade of the 'sixties, intimidation has taken on a new and menacing aspect, but we should not forget that if we delve into our history there were great intimidators of a ferocious aspect who terrified all with whom they came in contact and especially those who were in their power. Many of these great intimidators were faithful servants of the establishment of the day and carried out the orders of the king or of the Parliament with a zeal that knew no bounds. The archetype of this brand of great intimidator was George Jeffreys, known as Judge Jeffreys and made Baron Wem by James II.

Sir T. E. May, who knew a great deal about the privileges, proceedings and usage of Parliament, but perhaps less about lawyers as men, gives us the classic description of Judge Jeffreys in the following words.

'This execrable person, George Jeffreys, afterwards Baron Wem, was born at Acton in Denbighshire in 1648, entered Middle Temple in 1663, and was called to the bar in 1669. He was recorder of London, was knighted in 1678, became chief-justice of the country palatine of Chester in 1680, and was promoted to be chief-justice of the King's Bench in 1683. His subservience to the royal will was shown in his passing sentence on Algernon Sidney, 1683; and still more, on the accession of James II, when he made short work of the cases of Titus Oates and Baxter, and his reward was the peerage of Wem. James, happy in such a tool, sent him to try the rebels in the unhappy rising under the Duke of Monmouth, his brother and predecessor's illegitimate son; and he held out the seals as a further bribe to insure severity. Jeffreys well earned his reward in the terrible travesty of justice called the "Bloody Assize", or the "Bloody Circuit"; 350 rebels were hanged, over 800 were sold into slavery and sent to the West Indies and the American colonies, and the number of those whipped and imprisoned exceeds computation; while not only the judge, but the queen, the maids of honour, and other personages of the court, made large sums of money by the sale of pardons. Women were publicly whipped at the cart tail. Mrs. Lisle was beheaded at Winchester for harbouring a wounded rebel, although she was an aged lady universally beloved for her ready benevolence. Her late husband had been a lord of Cromwell's creation, and although the nobility of the Protectorate was not recognised at the Restoration, she was generally known as 'The lady Alice'. Indignation rose, but it increased into a deep hatred when the men saw the fires lit to burn Elizabeth Gaunt at the stake in Tyburn, for a like offence with good Mrs. Lisle. The "Bloody Assize" raged over August and September 1685, and at its close Jeffreys was made Lord Chancellor. In 1686 he was named head of the seven commissioners to govern the Church and at once began the persecution of the bishops, which in 1688 culminated in the prosecution of seven of them for libel, quickly followed by James' overthrow. Jeffreys endeavoured to escape in disguise, but was recognised by his bloated red face at Wapping, and dragged off by the populace. He was rescued by the trainbands, and taken to the Tower, 13th December 1688, the mob pursuing the carriage with howls of rage and fury; there he died on the 18th April following, 1689. He never recovered the terror of that dreadful night and its long procession, with the never-ceasing chance of a violent death. His fate had long been the subject of debate, and no death was thought bad enough for him, but meanwhile he drank heavily, and through that low means sunk under the universal opprobrium to a miserable end.'

This is at least a consistent portrait of a villain. Whether it is a substantially correct assessment of Jeffreys we shall perhaps never know. A number of modern writers, including the late Lord Birkenhead, have pointed out that Jeffreys had considerable intellectual abilities. George Jeffreys entered Trinity College, Cambridge, in March 1662, but stayed only a year because he was in a hurry to be taken into chambers, and an opportunity to do this occurred at that time, He was called to the Bar in 1668. Almost immediately he attracted the notice and the friendship of the most famous judge of the time, Sir Mathew Hale, Lord Chief Baron of the Exchequer and the greatest authority on criminal law living at that time. As Sir Mathew was a religious man of Puritan morality we may take it that George Jeffreys appeared to him to be a circumspect, well-mannered young man, leading a good life, a credit to the establishment.

George Jeffreys married twice and no criticism can be levelled against him as a husband. However, there is no doubt that the handsome young man was a ruthless legal adventurer who made friends with calculation among the rich merchants of the city of London. He did extremely well at the Bar, so that he was able to buy Bulstrode House, Buckinghamshire, where Charles II (who was accompanied by the Duchess of Portsmouth) dined with him. According to a newspaper report at the time, the king invited Jeffreys to be seated and drank his health several times. After this George Jeffreys was made. He was knighted and became Recorder of London, still a handsome man and not yet afflicted by the malady of the stone which caused him pain, which he attempted to drown by drinking great quantities of claret and porter. This habit, in his later years, gave him a bloated, scarlet appearance and seems to have added to the picture of cruel ferocity which at times was certainly justified.

As to the claim that Jeffreys was a major lawyer, this we must, I think, admit. In 1679, in cases arising out of the Popish Plot, Jeffreys was the first to proclaim it as a rule of law that the King's Proclamation took precedence over parliamentary petitions. As a result of his firm stand on behalf of the Crown in this matter, he was appointed Chief Justice of Chester. On the 12th May 1680 he was appointed Serjeant-at-Law, taking the motto *'a deo rex, a rege lex'*. Jeffreys was now permanently ranged on the side of the king against the Parliament. He was only thirty-five when he was appointed chief justice. Jeffreys greatly increased his reputation as a lawyer by his judgment in the famous 'Monopolies' case. But his lurid period as a great intimidator lay ahead.

We may take it that the attacks on Jeffreys by his political opponents the Whigs were incessant as soon as he became identified as a king's man, but it is fair to note that the volume entitled *State Trials* upon which much of the abuse of Jeffreys is founded was one of the most unreliable of the Whig compilations. The work was last published in 1811, but the first edition appeared in 1719, and differs very much from the Whig editions that followed it. If we were historians delving deeply into the matter we would have to distinguish between those accounts of trials over which Jeffreys presided, which were printed at the time, in which case they seem to have been verbatim and accurate, or those that were printed after the revolution and tended to be political tracts holding up Jeffreys to hatred, ridicule and contempt. We can take two examples of each category of report. The report of the trial of Titus Oates was made at the time and seems to be confirmed as being completely accurate, but the case of Pritchard versus Papillon, which took place in 1683, was first printed by Janeway in 1689. Janeway was a seditious journalist and added four pages of libellous abuse and scurrilous comment to his report of the case. So much so that when the *State Trial* series reprinted it these four pages were omitted as being obviously irrelevant and untrue.

So what we have here is a man who started life with every advantage, of which he made the fullest use. He had great gifts, a quick intellect, a profound grasp of legal theory, a facile tongue and limitless ambition. He was determined to carve his way to the top and he did so in a shorter time than anyone else has taken to achieve the same position before or since. As the late Lord Birkenhead himself became Lord

Chancellor at a very early age, he was perhaps conscious of the fact that only Jeffreys had beaten him in the legal race. In any case, Lord Birkenhead was right to point out that the true picture of Jeffreys was not totally black and that the terrible excesses of his last years were preceded by a period in which his brilliant gifts were manifest to his friends and enemies alike.

It was, of course, the rebellion of James, Duke of Monmouth, a favourite son of Charles II by his mistress, Lucy Walters, that led to the West Country Assize over which Jeffreys presided, hounding the rebels with his invective from the Bench and securing the death sentence to be passed on a large number of these unfortunate people.

The Duke of Monmouth was an engaging young man, profligate and extravagant, sensual and unscrupulous, but with a regal manner and deportment and a smile that captured the imagination of the crowd. He landed at Lyme Regis on the 11th June 1685 and was welcomed with open arms by the people of the West Country who had come to hate what they regarded as the tyranny of the Stuart kings.

James, Duke of Monmouth, had been spoiled from the start. As well as the title by which he was known, he was also created Duke of Orkney and, most unusually for an illegitimate son, he was made a Knight of the Garter. Twice in naval engagements against the Dutch, he displayed courage and initiative.

His private life would be regarded as exceptional even in the permissive society of today. He surrounded himself with young whores, ladies of fashion, Negro slaves, eunuchs and a curious assortment of animals, including some bad-tempered and hungry hounds whom he would unleash if anyone annoyed him. He treated his wife, a Scottish heiress, Anne Scott, the daughter of the Duke of Buccleuch, badly, often bringing his latest mistress into his house and even into his wife's bed. However, this side of his character was not generally known outside court circles, and in any case in seventeenth-century England it was not expected that the king or his family would behave like their subjects were expected to do.

Early in his career the young duke attracted those who feared a return to Catholicism under the Stuarts. He had been in trouble before because of political activities under the guidance of Lord Shaftesbury who arranged for him to make grand and triumphal tours of the country intended to whip up opposition to the Catholic menace. Out of these series of royal progresses the Rye House Plot was born. An eighteenth-century chronicler describes it as follows: 'This was a plot of the year 1683 to murder King Charles II and his brother James, Duke of York, afterwards James II, as they were returning to London from Newmarket races. It was only foiled by the royal party starting a week earlier than had been arranged. The plot is named from the meeting place of the conspirators, the Rye House farm on the Lee in Hertfordshire, not far from London, belonging to Rumbold a maltster, one of the conspirators.'

The plan was a simple one. A large cart was to be overturned and fired in the path of the royal progress, then the conspirators were to shoot the king, his brother and his entourage, escaping over the fields to initiate a rebellion aimed at the restoration of the Commonwealth. Fortunately for the king, some of the rebels who were captured were persuaded to confess and implicate their fellow conspirators. King Charles, as was his wont, quickly forgot the incident in spite of the terrible danger that awaited him had his party left Newmarket as originally planned, but the Duke of York never forgot. He was a more fearful and apprehensive type than King Charles and it was probably because he remembered the Rye House Plot that he refused the abject pleas of Monmouth to have his death sentence remitted.

Everywhere this handsome prince with his extraordinary charm and ease of manner was rapturously welcomed and in Taunton he was crowned King of England and was known from that day until his death as King Monmouth.

People flocked to the banner of the Duke of Monmouth so that he collected an army of some eight thousand men. Eventually they met the royal forces at Sedgemoor in Somerset. The royal army was about equal in numbers, but it was better led and better armed. For several hours the issue was in doubt and at one moment the followers of the duke thought that they had won and they had a vision of their leader proceeding in triumph to London. But the discipline and tenacity of the royal forces eventually led to the rout of the rebels. Monmouth was captured alive and put in the Tower. On the 15th of July he was executed by having his head cut off his body. He died, as he had lived, bravely. According to the custom of the day as a traitor his body would have been quartered, but the king ordered that it should be laid in a velvet coffin and he was buried privately.

The witch hunt was now on. The rebels, everywhere, in Somerset, in Dorset and in Devon, had to be smelled out. There was, of course, no doubt at all that the expedition and adventure of Monmouth had been treason of the highest order, for he had openly 'waged war against the king within his kingdom' so that the authorities had only to establish that a prisoner had in some way, however remote, aided or harboured the rebels, or had been identified with their cause or had spoken words in their favour to achieve an indictment for treason which the terrified jury might well accept as a reason for finding the prisoner guilty. When that had happened the judge could pass sentence of death either by burning, which was the ordinary method of killing traitors, or by hanging and quartering, or, in very minor cases, by flogging through the streets followed by deportation.

It was inevitable that the king should call upon his ally, Jeffreys, to head the Western Assize,

The whole Assize was indeed a bloody affair, between two and three hundred people being put to death and more than twice that number deported as slaves. But there was one case which will never be forgotten because it does reveal Jeffreys as a great and cunning intimidator, using his unbridled power to hound an old woman to her death. If we follow the case and read some of the interjections and comments of the judge it certainly seems as if Jeffreys in his last years had become a perverted sadist, who, often in pain himself and frequently under the influence of drink, though not drunk, indulged his appetite for terror which grew steadily worse as the Assize proceeded.

Lady Alice Lisle was the widow of Lord Commissioner Lisle, who had been one of the judges at the trial of Charles I which probably did not endear the family to the Stuarts. Her husband had sat in the House of Peers during the Commonwealth, but the creations of nobility made by Cromwell were not recognised after the Restoration, so there was at least some doubt as to the title of Alice Lisle. However, she was known as Lady Alice throughout the countryside in which she lived.

On August 27th, 1685, she appeared before Judge Jeffreys on the following charge: 'That on the 28th July, in the first year of King James II, knowing John Hicks of Keinsham, in the country of Somerset, clerk, to be a false traitor, and to have conspired the death and destruction of the King, and to have levied war against him, did, in her dwelling-house at Ellingham, traitorously entertain, conceal and comfort the said John Hicks, and cause meat and drink to be delivered to him, against the duty of her allegiance. . . .'

What had the prosecution to prove in order to substantiate this charge? They had to prove two facts, first they had to prove that Alice Lisle had entertained, concealed and comforted John Hicks and given him food and drink, and secondly they had to prove that she had done this knowing him to be a traitor who had levied war against the King with the intention of bringing about his death and destruction. I have read the original account of the trial and I think that the first charge cannot be denied. John Hicks was, in fact, accepted into the house of Alice Lisle and given food and water, or wine. He was 'harboured'. It is very doubtful whether Alice Lisle ever saw him, though the prosecution witnesses insisted that she did. What seems to me not to have been proved beyond all reasonable doubt was the fact that the old lady knew or realised that he was a fugitive from the battle of Sedgemoor. She herself, of course, was not allowed to give evidence on oath but she made a statement saying that she knew nothing of this at all, that she had been told that there was a man in the stables who was a debtor running away from his creditors and that that was all she knew of the matter.

L

However, Jeffreys was certainly out to convict and hang Alice Lisle. He refreshed himself that morning before going on to the Bench with a pint of claret, a dose he repeated at midday. This had the effect of killing his pain for the time being, but it also probably increased his ferocity and accounts for the extraordinary language he used towards the prisoner and witnesses. Alice Lisle was at this time nearly eighty years of age. She was silver-haired, frail and almost deaf. No pity of any kind seems to have moved Jeffreys, who hunted her throughout the trial with an implacable hatred.

To prove that Hicks had taken part in the rebellion the prosecution called a man named Charles Pope who gave the following evidence:

"'I had the misfortune to be taken prisoner by Monmouth's army", said the witness. "I was brought to Keinsham, and put into Sir Thomas Bridge's stables, and kept under a guard there. Hicks came and asked after the prisoners, who were four or five in number, and asked if we were kindly used. We said that we had had but a small piece of bread in two days. Hicks replied that he was sorry for it and said he would speak to the King (meaning the Duke of Monmouth). There was a gentleman with him called the King's chaplain. Mr. Hicks also told us the King (Monmouth) was a good Protestant; and he wondered what we could say for ourselves being Protestants, in serving a Popish prince and not obeying a Protestant King; and used several other expressions reflecting on the King and Government."'

This evidence was confirmed by two other witnesses Fitzherbert and Taylor. Of course, the fact that Hicks had fought in the rebellion was not really in dispute in relation to the Lisle case. What was in dispute was whether Alice Lisle knew of this.

Mr. Polexfen, the counsel for the Crown, then called James Dunne to prove that Alice Lisle had harboured Hicks knowing him to be a traitor. Dunne from the start appeared to be a most reluctant witness and Polexfen asked that he might be examined 'strictly' which these days we would express in terms of being a hostile witness.

However, this was not sufficient for Jeffreys, who urged

Dunne to consider both his temporal and spiritual affairs and said that if he told lies he would very soon be found out adding: 'None of your saints can save your soul; neither shall they save your body if I catch you prevaricating. I will punish every variation from the truth I find you guilty of.' As Mr. Dunne had not yet given a word in evidence this seems to be a prejudiced and sinister warning and it certainly was intimidation of a witness by a judge which today would certainly cause the Court of Appeal to order a new trial.

Dunne was a reasonably brave man, but he was terrified by Jeffreys. When the judge had spoken of his 'temporal affairs' he had meant all his property which might be forfeited to the Crown if he was found by perjury to have assisted a traitor. It was an open threat of imprisonment, ruin and perhaps even death. This Dunne could not withstand. He was not a martyr and he gave, more or less, the evidence that the judge was demanding but he did contrive to slip in some remarks designed to help Alice Lisle.

He had gone to the house of Lady Lisle on a Saturday where he had met her bailiff, Carpenter. Dunne had asked Carpenter if he thought that Alice Lisle would take Hicks into her house. Carpenter said he did not know but he would take a message to her. Lady Lisle sent a message back saying that Hicks might come on Tuesday in the evening. Jeffreys asked if Lady Lisle had enquired whether Dunne knew Hicks, but the witness said he did not remember. He also said that he did not know whether Lady Lisle was acquainted with Hicks. Judge Jeffreys said: 'Would she entertain one she had no knowledge of, merely upon thy message?' To which Dunne replied: 'My Lord, I tell you the truth. On the Tuesday morning about seven o'clock three of them came to my house, a little black man and a full black man and a thin black man. I knew none of their names. About eleven o'clock we set out and a man named Barter showed us the way.'

When the party arrived at the house of Alice Lisle, Hicks went in and the witness did not see him again until he was arrested. They left their horses at the gate but Dunne put his in the stable. Jeffreys, who was as quick as a viper in striking at points that helped his case, asked: 'Was the stable door locked or open?' But he was told that it was latched.

From this point onwards the witness roused the full fury of the judge. When the judge asked him to say upon his oath who had opened the stable door, the witness or Carpenter, Dunne replied: 'It was Carpenter, my lord.'

Judge Jeffreys then exploded into the following words: 'Why, thou vile wretch! Didst thou not tell me that thou didst pull up the latch? But, it seems, the Saints have a charter for lying; they may lie, and cant, and deceive, and rebel, and think God Almighty takes no notice of it. A Turk has a better title to an eternity of bliss than these pretenders to Christianity, for he has more morality and honesty in him. Sirrah! I charge you, in the presence of God, tell me true: what other persons did you see that night?'

Dunne was now on the run, so to speak, and the judge hounded him with unconcealed ferocity. At the end of Dunne's evidence the judge exclaimed: 'Thou art a strange prevaricating, shuffling, snivelling, lying rascal! Does the prisoner wish to ask him any questions?' Alice Lisle did not hear the judge, but when his question was repeated to her she said that she had no questions to ask. Jeffreys' comment on this was: 'Perhaps your questions might endanger the truth coming out.'

A man called Barker was called and said that he saw Dunne hand a letter to the bailiff at Alice Lisle's house. When this evidence was given the judge called Dunne back saying: 'Let honest Mr. Dunne stand forth a little. You carried a message from Hicks to my Lady Lisle; did you not also carry a letter?' But Dunne resolutely denied having done so which led the judge to say: 'How hard the truth comes out of a lying Presbyterian knave! Consider the oath thou hast taken; that thou are in the presence of a God that cannot endure a lie and thou hast called him to witness what thou dust testify, the truth, the whole truth and nothing but the truth.'

When, in answer to another question, Dunne hesitated before replying, the judge really let his fury rip: 'What an age do we live in! What a generation of vipers do we live among!

Sirs, is this what you call the Protestant religion? Thou wicked wretch, I charge you once more as you will answer it at the bar of the great judge, answer my question.'

Eventually Dunne broke down saying: 'I am so confounded that I know not what I say myself. Tell me what you would have me say, for I am nearly out of my senses.' But the judge would have none or this. 'Harkee, man, here nobody confounds thee; it is thy own depraved heart that confounds both thy honesty and understanding. It is thy studying how to prevaricate that puzzles and confounds thy intellect.'

The judge ordered that a candle should be held up to the face of the witness (it was getting dark) 'so that all could see the lying countenance of this wretched man.'

In the end Jeffreys ordered an information of perjury to be served against Dunne.

Colonel Penruddock gave evidence that he had surrounded the house of Alice Lisle and taken her prisoner when she had been charged with harbouring Hicks. As the trial seemed to be now coming to an end, Lady Lisle said: 'I hope I shall not be condemned without being heard.' To which Jeffreys replied: 'God forbid! That was the practice in your husband's time, but not now.' The remark clearly shows the malice which Jeffreys and his master the king had against the house of Lisle.

Lady Lisle then made a statement to the court, part of which read as follows: 'My Lord, I am told that I ought not to be tried for harbouring a traitor till that traitor is convicted. Besides, I will take my death upon it, I never knew of Nelthorp's coming until he came. Had I heard this name I should have remembered it being in the proclamation. As to what they say to my denying Nelthorp being in my house, I was in great consternation and dread of the soldiers, who were very rude and could not be restrained by their officers from plundering my house. I beg your Lordship will not harbour an ill opinion of me from these false reports that go about me concerning my consenting to the death of King Charles the First; for I was not out of my chamber the day he was beheaded, and believe I shed more tears for him than any woman then living did, as the Countess of Monmouth, my Lady Marlborough, my Lord Chancellor Hyde, and twenty other persons of quality could have witnessed. As I hope to attain salvation, I did not know Nelthorp before in my life. I was indeed willing to shelter Hicks, knowing him to be a dissenting preacher, and that there were warrants out against him on that account . . . I beseech your Lordship to believe that I had no design to harbour him, but as a Nonconformist, which I knew was no treason, nor can it be supposed that I would venture the ruin of myself and children to harbour Nelthorp, whom I never knew, but had heard he was in the proclamation.'

Alice Lisle, in the face of death, probably by burning, stood her ground and insisted that she had not known that the man Hicks had any connection with the rebellion whatever.

On the legal point that had been raised, the jury enquired of the judge whether it was proper to proceed against the prisoner before the rebel she was said to have harboured had been convicted of treason. The Lord Chief Justice replied that it was the same as if the man had died of his wounds before being convicted. This appears to be a very specious answer if, indeed, it did answer the question at all. The jury then retired and came back in half an hour, the foreman saying: 'My Lord, we have some doubt whether she knew Hicks had been in the Army.' To which the judge replied: 'Did she not enquire of Dunne if Hicks was in the Army? And when he told her he did not know she did not say she would refuse him, but ordered him to come by night, by which it is evident that she suspected it; and did not he and Nelthorp discourse of the battle and the Army when they were at supper. Come, come, gentlemen, it is plain proof. But if there was no such proof, the circumstances and management of the thing is as full of proof as can be. I wonder what it is you doubt of.'

After this final admonition the jury found Alice Lisle guilty as charged.

On August 28th, 1685, Alice Lisle was brought to the Bar to receive sentence together with a number of common criminals.

In his speech passing sentence the judge showed that ferocity had now given way to hypocrisy. He pronounced her a convicted traitor and that she should be burned. However, he said that if she would confess the execution would be delayed. Alice Lisle made no confession but two of the bishops at Winchester managed to reprieve the matter until the 2nd of September. King James was petitioned that the form of execution should be altered to beheading. The king allowed this and Alice Lisle was beheaded in the market place at Winchester on the 2nd of September. She died with unflinching courage, handing mementoes to those who were near and dear to her.

Looking at the case as a whole it was certainly not proved that Alice Lisle knew that Hicks had been a soldier in the rebel army, though she may possibly have suspected it. However, she was not charged with harbouring a man whom she suspected might have been a rebel, but with knowing that he was a rebel and a traitor. With regard to the conversation at the supper table, as Alice Lisle practically heard nothing that anybody said, it was doubtful whether she heard any references to the battle or the fighting that may have been made.

It came out later that Jeffreys had done a deal with the witness Nelthorp for the trial, making sure that his evidence would bolster up the case of the Crown. After the revolution of 1688 the judgment on Lady Lisle was annulled by Act of Parliament and the forfeited property returned to her family.

So what is our verdict? It must be that although various types of intimidation exist and seem to multiply today, at least we have no judge on the Bench who is as diabolical and ferocious an intimidator as George Jeffreys who rightly is remembered in history as the ogre of the Bloody Assize.

14

The Summing-up

A<small>LL</small> authors, when they have finished a book, have to consider the reaction to it of the public who are the jury in the case and who decide whether it is a good, a bad, or an indifferent book. All kinds of considerations will influence their judgment.

Does the author really know his subject? Has he expressed his views and put forward the facts clearly and attractively? Has the personality of the author as a human being come across so that each reader feels, at least to some extent, a shared sympathy? Has the author shown a wide enough vision and experience to express not only the subject itself but its ambiance and the consequences and results it may provoke?

I must say that, when I set out the criteria like this, I feel some alarm. Very few writers, I imagine, measure up to all these standards. And they do give rise to a great many questions. For instance, to what extent in a book of this kind should an author allow his personality and private convictions to enter into the story?

When I started to write sixteen years ago the critics tended to say: 'We could do with a lot less Gerald Sparrow.' But recently and, to me, surprisingly, they have attributed the modest success of my books to the fact that I cannot resist getting in touch with my readers, even popping out of the format from time to time and speaking to them directly. Perhaps in our current permissive age even this is now permitted. The fact of the matter is that I like people and it is very difficult for me to be impersonal.

Suppose that we allow this personalised approach, we will still demand of our authors a certain degree of objectivity and a lack of prejudice. But well-established and chronic convictions are part of the harvest we gather as we go along. Moreover, it is a fact that prejudice is a word only currently used to describe those who disagree with the permissive, revolutionary, and fashionable thought of today. Any undergraduate can get up and tell me that he could run the Republic of South Africa better than the government of that country, but if I venture to disagree with him, I am prejudiced, probably a Fascist and one of the first to qualify for imprisonment when the day of freedom dawns.

Moreover, if I advance my views with urbanity that is a crime in itself, it is merely an exercise in the decadent upper-class 'charm' that was used to lull the people into accepting less than their slice of the cake.

I am not complaining. I welcome the fact that in public life we now have a wide and desperate cleavage between those who want to preserve and those who think it necessary to destroy. At least the great debate is not trivial. Its effect will determine the future of every man, woman and child.

What have we been saying in *The Great Intimidators*?

We start, I suppose, with the premise that fear is an innate and universal instinct. We acknowledge that power-seeking or simply greedy people recognise this weakness and are prepared to exploit it—to use intimidation either to enrich themselves or to achieve political aims.

We follow this up with the hopeful thesis that Western democracy is based on the negation of fear. To us it is vitally important that Western democracy should survive and be strong for this reason.

In a free and democratic world intimidation should be a dying industry. But it is not. I take a pessimistic view of this matter. I do not think that our democratic Europe will exist in ten years' time, both France and Italy having fallen by the wayside. And I see no sign whatever that increasing personal prosperity has led to a decrease in crime, whether involving intimidation or not.

Perhaps the erosion of faith has something to do with this. When people believed in God they felt they had nothing to fear. It may all have been an illusion, but it was an effective illusion. The Christian was fortified against all comers. The cases in this book have introduced a number of evil men, men who were not bound by any morality, any restraint. We moan about our empty churches but seldom seek the cause of the current disbelief. Political priests, lack of piety, poverty, and chastity may have something to do with it. The young in particular admire dedication to an ideal. They are not seeking an efficient parish organiser, however useful such a person is.

Fear, of course, breeds fear and the materialism of life now encourages fear. If money is the only real criterion, then the tendency must be to fear being left behind in the race for that commodity. Modern advertisement recognises this and exploits every kind of personal fear. Fear of growing old, fear of sexual impotence, fear of body-odour, fear of being left behind by the couple next door who have three cars, two refrigerators (one deep), a variety of washing-up machines and—inevitably—wall-to-wall carpeting.

Fear arises from an acute apprehension of danger and there is one kind of fear that none of us can now escape—the fear of total destruction by a nuclear war. The roots of the word fear show the connection with danger clearly: the old English word *faer* being derived from the German *gefahr,* which simply meant danger.

The odd feature of the whole appalling scene is that, knowing our danger and feeling our fear, we have done virtually nothing about it. The abolition of nuclear weapons, once thought a possibility and desirable, is now regarded as pure wishful thinking. We shall have to live, we are told, by the balance of terror. What rubbish. We should at least try to save ourselves while there is yet time.

Apathy is the real danger. The attitude: 'We cannot change it, so why bother?' Out of the monstrosities of current society fear breeds; the intimidators are given the opportunity to ply their malignant sorcery.

When the time comes to say goodbye to readers of a book I always feel a sense of sorrow which is, I suppose, irrational. Even sentimental. But why not? What is wrong with senti-ment? The heart of man will be there when our pragmatic, computerised society has torn itself to bits and been exposed as a sham and a shambles.

I hoped you liked the two chapters with an Eastern setting: 'Charley Lester and his *Nacklengs*' and 'The Grasshopper'. The East always plays its own melody and writes its own lyrics.

We have probed together a fascinating subject. It has enthralled me—and I hope it has not bored you.

Index

ATHERSLEY BRANCH